IN BED
WITH
AN
ELEPHANT

IN BED
WITH
AN
ELEPHANT

CHARLES NEILSON GATTEY

Rosters Ltd

Published by ROSTERS LTD
60 Welbeck St, London, W1.

© Charles Neilson Gattey
ISBN 0-948032-54-5

Designed and published by ROSTERS
Typeset in Century Schoolbook
by JH Graphics Ltd, Reading

Printed and bound in Great Britain by
Cox and Wyman Ltd, Reading, Berks

First edition 1989

To Eve Blackburn

Contents

INTRODUCTION:
THE BEST MEDICINE

Mae West sang in one of her musicals that the mother of
a certain character ought to have thrown him away and
kept the stork. This is a jest that has a degree of under-
lying truth in it as some receive more attention and affection from the animals they keep as pets than from their
nearest relatives.

George Eliot wrote in *Mr Gilfil's Love Story* 'Animals
are such agreeable friends — they ask no questions, they
pass no criticisms.' Walt Whitman believed them better
than humans to live with because they were 'so placid and
self-contained' and 'not demented with the mania of owning things'.

Elizabeth Barrett Browning expressed her experience
with Flush thus:

> But of *thee* it shall be said,
> This dog watched beside a bed
> Day and night unweary,
> Watched within a curtained room,
> When no sunbeam brake the gloom
> Round the sick and dreary.
>
> Roses, gathered for a vase,
> In that chamber died apace,
> Beam and breeze resigning;
> This dog only, waited on,

Knowing that when light is gone
Love remains for shining.

Coming to more recent times, that sex symbol also
famous as the 'Madonna of the Strays', Brigitte Bardot,
revealed to a journalist that at the height of her career
she was petrified to go out. 'I couldn't make a move – I
was in hiding as though I was on the run from the police.
I felt as though I were trapped and hung in a cage. That
was when I realised how naturally good animals are.
They gave me kindness and love which is more that I can
say about people!'

Actress Beryl Reid is famous for her collection of cats
and she claims to have found them to be the most effective
relievers of tension and that the act of stroking one
'brings down the blood pressure and lessens the likelihood
of heart attacks or nervous breakdowns.'

In the United States, at the Oakwood Forensic Centre
in Lima, Ohio, it was found that when those habitually
violent, including hardened criminals, were made to live
for a time in the company of animals the reformative
effect on them was extraordinary. There were 150 small
pets such as canaries, cockateels, gerbils, guinea pigs,
macaws, mynah birds, parakeets, parrots, and rabbits.
Those taking part in this experiment were also given the
duty of looking after ducks, geese, goats, deer, peacocks,
and cats. This 'Pet Therapy Program' was the brain child
of David Lee, a psychiatric social worker, who has thus
demonstrated that such intimate association with
animals can cure far more successfully than conventional
treatments. The responsibility and pleasure of having a
pet for a friend is usually a new experience that completely changes outlooks on life.

Some six years ago, Dorothy Walster of the Scottish
Health Education group published the results of her
investigations into what extent the company of an animal
enriched the lives of the over sixties as well as preventing

their health deteriorating. After studying the evidence assembled, she reached a similar conclusion to David Lee's — that an alternative therapy to that received from medical practitioners can be found in pet ownership. Animals, she pointed out, are often close to their owners both day and night and require little attention. People who otherwise would have lost interest in life became mentally stimulated. The lonely gained the presence of friends to whom they could talk. Those who were cold had something to cuddle that kept continually warm — unlike a hot water bottle — and cost nothing — unlike an electric blanket. Those who felt suicidal were given an incentive for living. The message was clear, people with pets live longer because they realise that they are essential to the continued welfare and happiness of the animals in their care.

1

THE GOOD LIFE

Ronald Reagan, when Governor of California, was a client of the Canine Behaviour Institute of Beverley Hills where experts psychoanalysed dogs afflicted with depression or any form of neurosis at a cost of about $3,000, requiring six visits accompanied by owners. Their presence was obligatory, for the Institute maintained that it was not the pet's responsibility to appreciate the wishes of its owner but the reverse.

In England now there are similar services for cats. The *Daily Telegraph* for January 24, 1989, told its readers that owners concerned about the mental welfare of their pets would be pleased to learn of a feline behavioural clinic just founded by a vet in Addlestone, Surrey. Peter Neville was well qualified for this, given that he wrote about cat behaviour in *Cat World*, the leading publication for ailurophiles. He specialised in the treatment of agoraphobia, depression, aggression and incontinence, believing that cats were 'sensitive souls who can develop plenty of problems'. Persians, Burmese and Siamese were his most difficult patients, apart from uncastrated toms which he had found to be 'devils if they're frustrated'.

* * *

It is a pity that Mr Neville's work does not include treating parrots for he might have been able to help a Derbyshire family with their problem cockatiel. A week earlier, the *Daily Telegraph* reported how they had been forced to buy a new telephone because their pet was so good at impersonating the old one. Kenneth Miles said his wife and son were tired of jumping up to answer the phone, only to find their bird making the ringing noise. He added: 'We even named him Buzby, but he calls himself Joey, so we had to come round to his way of thinking.'

The account ends: 'The bird now listens intently when the new phone rings, and the family fear he may be rehearsing the new tone in secret.'

* * *

In *The Pet Connection: its Influence on our Health and Quality of Life*, Helen T Kelley and Robert M Kidd discussed reports about a study which explored the possibilities of matching pets other than cats and dogs to owners' personality types for physical and psychological benefits. The results showed, for example, that male horse owners were aggressive and dominant while female ones were easy-going and non-agressive. Owners of turtles were hard-working, reliable and 'upwardly mobile', while those of birds were 'socially outgoing and expressive'.

Star struck

It is perhaps only to be expected that pet owners who are addicted to astrology and pry into the future through palmistry should be intrigued to know what is in store for their canine Capricorn or pussy Pisces. There is a busy clairvoyant in Brighton who reads paws, feeling the vibrations coming through them, as well as casting 'Doggie' and 'Kitty' horoscopes – and counselling on the right sign of the zodiac for the mate of stately spaniel Sophie or boisterous retriever Rosie.

There are books, too, that can be consulted such as Liz Tresilian's *Sun-Signs for Cats*. Librans, we learn, love humans except stingy people who keep the heating low, and their perfect owners should be born under Aquarius or Gemini. Scorpios do anything for excitement. Females bring their mates back for cream teas, are choosy and would rather remain single than end up with Mr Wrong. Signs for ideal guardians – Aries and Leo. Capricorn cats are snobs and if they ignore owners (Taurus or Virgo most suitable) it is because they think them common. Aquarians often have Roman noses, chase dogs, go out in the rain, make pals with the mice – do the opposite of what the normal cat is supposed to do. They get on best with Libra and Gemini folk.

Pisces pussies love water and often go to sleep in the bath. They are happiest on board ship with a Captain born under Cancer or Scorpio. The Aries mog is wilful and reckless and is happiest roaming about on a farm. Only someone whose sign is Sagittarius can control him. Taurus felines are born lazy, sleeping all day in your favourite chair, loving food and children as well as owners born under Capricorn or Virgo. The Gemini cat is possessive and playful, and enjoys most a randy night out. Not the pet for the house-proud and needs an Aquarian or Libra to master him or her, while a psychiatrist born under Pisces or Scorpio is required to fathom the crazy, mixed-up Cancer cat which leads a lonesome sex life.

King of cats is the one whose sign is Leo who, if he cannot live in the lap of luxury, will stalk out. Sex is the only thing he does not consider beneath him. The females, too, will stoop to conquer. You ought to be a Sagittarian or an Arian to cope with such a pet. But have for companion a Virgoan cat if you want one whose main objects in life are to please you, to respect your carpets, never to claw the furniture and is always washing. It is only when the females are in the family-way that you may find them in the airing cupboard having kittens on your clothes. Liz Tresilian says that, in this case, the ideal combination calls for an owner born under Capricorn or Taurus.

Food for thought

If Mrs 'Pat' Campbell were alive today, she might well entrust the care of Moonbeam whilst she was abroad to some caring experts such as the Elmwood Exclusive Kennels at Great Missenden, Bucks, voted the best in the world for the third year running by the American Boarding Kennels Association and run by John Burton. To ensure high standards, he takes only ten dogs at a time, charging £150 a week. For this a dog is given his own centrally-heated room, fresh flowers daily, individual menus and colour TV.

In a *Sunday Express* feature, Jenny Nisbet described her visit to this Pooch's Palace. Breakfast consisted of Weetabix, bacon and sausage. Lunch was the main meal. One had steak, chips and fresh salmon; the others beef and tripe. Four drank champagne, and one *crème de menthe* because he was accustomed to having a tot after dinner at home with his master. 'And we always use a marg blessed by the Rabbi when frying steak for our Jewish dogs,' revealed Mr Burton. 'At bedtime some have Horlicks with a drop of rum in it. They enjoy going to bed with a fresh marrow bone and they love it when Julie-Ann reads them a story. We have a baby alarm directly above our own bed, so we hear the moment anything's wrong. But I did draw the line when one owner wanted his dog to sleep between me and my wife. I said, "How are we going to carry on normal married life?" The man's wife turned all huffy and said, "Well, my husband and I seem to manage it." '

John Burton further disclosed that he often had to get dogs out of their rooms to come to the telephone. 'They ring them from Barbados, ask if they're having a nice time and so on. Or they send postcards, which, of course, we read out. Some have little lace-up shoes which look quite smart walking about in town. But they don't need them here.' Just velvet slippers, embroidered in gold with their initials, no doubt.

* * *

Neville Whitaker in his book, *Animals By Air*, relates how an extremely rich couple living in the Bahamas died and left their Peke, Fifi, to their nurse, Maria, an Austrian girl, together with financial provision for its upkeep and instructions that the dog should always be given the finest veterinary treatment available anywhere in the world when needed. This arising, Maria brought it by air to Heathrow where it had to spend 48 hours in quarantine before being transferred to the Hackbridge Kennels for dental treatment. Maria would not hear of Fifi being fed on hostel food and arranged with the Aerial Hotel to send over their menus. On the chef's personal recommendation, she chose Chicken Kiev followed by Boeuf Stroganoff for its lunch and *Agneau Rôti* Aerial Hotel for dinner. Whitaker comments that he wondered how a dog with toothache that had travelled thousands of miles to have it put right could cope with such fare.

* * *

In their book, *All Gourmets Great and Small*, Clive and Angela Russell-Taylor described the diets of various pets belonging to showbiz personalities. Katie Boyle's dogs, Baba and Bizzie, rescued from the Battersea Dogs' Home, must feel that they have entered paradise. The former, who has a liking for savouries, enjoys Camembert, whilst the latter prefers soft Italian chocolates called Gianduiottis. Their main dish consists of tinned food mixed with chicken and fish to which in winter is added a few drops of Abidec, a children's vitamin complex. In summer this mixture has grated carrot and chopped spinach, both raw, added to it.

* * *

Carla Lane, author of such top TV situation comedies as *Bread*, proves that a busy person can always find time for doing more. Her two tortoises are fed on baby food, her rabbits on muesli and parrot food, her wolfhound, Maximus, prefers bananas to bones and eats a pot full of honey a week, and her 36 birds love fresh pea-pods and cucumber. Carla also looks after four cats: Wolfgang likes cottage cheese with pineapple; Pandora adores Flora margarine on all her food; and Sorrow insists on goldfish food being sprinkled over her grub. They turn up their

18

noses at saucers of milk but lap up greedily melted ice cream, and have a passion for avocado.

* * *

Ernie Wise's poodle, Charlie, lived happily for the whole of his long life on a diet of raw mince and Brie, whilst the brindle Scottie, Hannibal Boots, who toured with him in the early days, liked to have a tin of strained carrots poured over his biscuits with an onion on the side.

* * *

There are few large towns nowadays in Britain without a pets' supermarket. Catering for them has become a thriving industry. Already in May, 1985, Jan Etherington in the *Sunday Express* was commenting on this. For vegetarians averse to giving their dogs meat bones there was an alternative in Bran Bones, the high fibre health treat. Among the canine toys were chocolate-scented squeaky bananas and a similarly scented rubber foot with red toenails, while cats might be given to nibble tasty Cat Love treats or furry mice to play with. Cellophane-wrapped locusts were for gerbils to lunch on, before which to work up an appetite they might gambol with a guaranteed chew-resistant play ball. The Observe-A-Bird kit enabled you to get near enough to a sparrow to drench him with Plume Spray, a grooming aid.

* * *

In the United States, catering for pets is on a vaster scale. At the International Conference on the Human—Companion Animal Bond held at the University of Pennsylvania in October, 1981, it was reported that 4 billion dollars were spent annually in the country to feed some 48 million dogs, 27 million cats, 25 million birds, 250 million fish, and 125 million other assorted captive animals. And the Humane Society was cited as estimating that over 3,000 cats and dogs were born every hour in the States, and that household pets consumed approximately 3.5 million tons of food each year.

Marital discord

Sometimes marital disputes over pets can lead to the husband moving out, such as in the case covered in the *Daily Telegraph* for January 30, 1989. Chris Tighe reported that while Mrs Freda Appleby's 85 stripy cats, tabby cats, tortoiseshell cats and black and white ones enjoyed the run of her bungalow, her husband, Stanley, lived in a caravan at the bottom of the garden. He had been back inside the two-bedroom bungalow near Pickering, Yorkshire, only once since leaving ten years previously – and that was to use the telephone.

Fifty-four year old Mrs Appleby, nine years younger than Stanley and who had no children, said: 'He won't come back – well, there's no room for him. I love my husband. He's a kind man and he's tolerant, but not enough to live with all these cats. I suppose they've become my family.'

Mrs Appleby found the money for meeting the cats' £45 a week food bill through working as a car park warden. Her passion for the animals began in the 1960s when her husband bought her a Persian kitten.

Dr Buster Lloyd-Jones in *The Animals Came In One By One* wrote about a big black poodle called Fifi, around whose life his mistress's own was so centred that she forced her husband to give up his war-time meat ration to feed the animal. In addition, he had to buy the lease of the flat next door so that Fifi could have a separate bedroom and bathroom. Eventually, the husband told his better half that she must choose between the poodle and himself. She chose the former.

But it is not always, of course, the husband who is thus treated like a second fiddle. A woman divorced her spouse because of his love for a 5-foot long boa constrictor. He had insisted on having the pet to sleep in bed with them – nearly always coiled around him. Should she complain that the snake scared her, he would shout and sometimes strike her. The only time she felt safe was when he was at work and the snake snoozed in a closed wicker basket, but the moment he returned, it was released and he had it coiled around his neck and shoulders as they sat at the table eating the evening meal. The last straw for her was when he started feeding it with live mice. She obtained a divorce on the grounds of mental cruelty. Once they were apart, he bought another boa with the intention of breeding them.

The saluki was the royal dog of ancient Egypt and the Bedouins regard them as precious as a blood horse. One Arab chief exchanged two dozen of his wives for an exceptionally well-bred one.

. . . and affection

However, when both husband and wife love the same kind of strange pet, it can lead to great happiness, as in the case of a Californian college professor who married a

student sharing his passion for alligators. They bought a
baby one to keep in their apartment where it would sleep
in a special bed and be first in the bath every morning.
After getting a lot of fun watching it splashing about in
the water, they would dry it with its very own towel and
leave it in the living-room listening to taped music. When
not at college, the couple would take the alligator out for
its favourite form of recreation — bumping about on the
back seat of their car.

2

PETS OF FANCY LADIES

Ninon de l'Enclos, the celebrated seventeenth century courtesan, who had her last love affair when well over eighty, was devoted to her pet, Raton, who looked more like a porcelain ornament than a dog. Striped black and white like a zebra and with a tail resembling that of a squirrel, he was no larger than a rat and always sat beside her at dinner parties, when his behaviour would be impeccable until dessert was served. Then, according to Fréville in his *Histoire des Chiens Célèbres*, he would run to and fro on the table, greeting the guests and receiving 'kisses and macaroons'. But the moment liqueurs appeared, he would seize his mistress's glass and run away to hide it in his basket. If she obtained another and tried to help herself, Raton would start to bark and, should she persist, his disapproval became louder and louder much to the company's merriment.

'Doctor,' Ninon would say, 'you will at least allow me to have a drink of water?' At these words, all barking ceased and Raton's tail wagged approvingly as he sipped from the same goblet as his mistress. 'Then,' Fréville wrote, 'he would nibble a biscuit and dance a minuet or two for the further entertainment of the guests.'

Going for gold

Madame de Pompadour, mistress of King Louis XV, was the first person in France to own a goldfish, which had been brought to her as a rare gift from China. Cynics commented that it was a most suitable pet for her as she had fished so much gold from her royal lover. It became the fashion for other courtesans to have goldfish for pets, their merits being that they were highly decorative and, being silent and confined, did not become jealous and attack lovers as other types might have done. In the late 1770s, Count von Heyden, the Prussian Ambassador to Holland, brought the first goldfish to Berlin as a present to a lady friend. A decade later, in his imposing winter garden at St Petersburg, Prince Potemkin held a birthday banquet for his mistress, the Tsarina Catherine, and adorned every table with the now much esteemed goldfish from far-off China disporting themselves in crystal bowls.

In France, during the First Empire, courtesans made it high fashion for women to array themselves with tiny goldfish swimming in spherical glass containers suspended from ear-rings.

It was in 1711 that goldfish were first seen in Europe when a ship belonging to the Duke of Richmond brought to England a large earthenware vessel full of live goldfish from China, where ever since about AD 960 they had been kept as domestic pets. Golden, silver, red, black and speckled varieties in elegant garden ponds were everywhere to be seen three hundred years later.

According to a Chinese legend, the first goldfish appeared in 771 BC during the reign of the Emperor P'ing. There had been a drought for over three months and the people in despair sacrificed to the gods. Then suddenly in a temple, water gushed up from the ground and the people saw a glittering goldfish leaping about in it, and rain started to pour from the heavens.

Surprisingly enough, goldfish were unknown in the United States until the 1870s. During the last war, what proved to be the most popular species of all was introduced — a coal-black veil-tail called Old Black Joe after Stalin, which became the advertising emblem for marketing 'Liberty bonds'.

* * *

Frances Stuart, Duchess of Richmond, was not only a mistress of King Charles II, but also the model for the original Britannia on English coins. Her pet for forty years was a grey parrot which could mimic the King's laughter and her crying and which died shortly after her in 1702. The stuffed bird, resting on her wax effigy, was placed in Westminster Abbey.

* * *

Arguably the most successful courtesan in Paris during the Second Empire was an Englishwoman, born in Plymouth, who called herself Cora Pearl. A certain Comte Aguado got to know her in a rather unconventional way. He owned a Havana bitch and wanted to find a mate for her. Learning that Cora had a Havana dog named Loulou, he visited her and found that she had dyed the pet blue to match her dress. This must have enhanced the sex appeal of both, for a canine and a human liaison blossomed.

Doggy dilemmas

The Contessa di Castiglione, one of the most beautiful women of her time, was mistress of both the Emperor Napoleon III and King Victor Emmanuel II of Italy, in addition to the 4th Marquis of Hertford and Baron James de Rothschild. But she was fond most of all of her two pet dogs, Kasino and Sandouga, whom she taught to waltz. In accordance with her last wishes, she was interred clad in the nightgown she had worn at Compiègne the night she first had sex with the Emperor – and with the two dogs stuffed and placed at her feet in the coffin.

On the first Napoleon's wedding night with Josephine, her dog, Fortune, was in bed with them. Later, he revealed: 'I had to choose between sleeping beside the beast or not sleeping with my wife. A terrible dilemma, but I had to take it or leave it. I resigned myself. The dog was less accommodating. I have the marks on my leg to show what he thought about the matter.'

* * *

Lillie Langtry at the height of her love affair with Edward VII, then Prince of Wales, had a parrot for a pet. When the news spread that it had escaped from her house, a gossip-writer wrote: 'That the lady possesses such a bird we were unaware, but we know she had a cockatoo.'

* * *

Princess Mathilde, the Emperor Napoleon III's cousin,

lived apart from her husband and had an ardent lover, the Count Niewekerke. This was common knowledge, but never mentioned in polite society. No one was supposed to know about it. One afternoon, when the Princess was entertaining ladies in her Paris salon, her pet dog, a miniature greyhound, bounded over to her hoping to be hugged. But, instead, she wagged a reproving finger at it, saying: 'Don't you know I'm cross with you, you bad boy?' Then, turning to her guests, she explained: 'Last night he kept leaping on my bed and I couldn't sleep.' Shortly afterwards, the Count arrived and the dog rushed up to him, but he, too, wagged a finger at it, and groused: 'You're a nuisance and I'm still angry with you. Jumping on the bed all night and keeping me awake.'

Pet alibi

Coming to this century, Jilly Cooper tells how a heavily made-up harridan called at the Battersea Dogs' Home hoping to find there a brown and white terrier that she had lost. She went round with the keeper and was over-joyed when such a dog suddenly started barking frantically in its pen and pounded the bars. Tears of joy welled into the woman's eyes 'until her rouge and her purple mascara streaked down her cheeks and both her false eyelashes fell off'.

'Forgive my curiosity,' said the keeper, letting the woman have the happy animal, 'but you don't look the sort of person who'd break down over an old mongrel.'

'Well,' replied the lady, 'the little bugger's my bread and butter, ain't he? I'm on the game, you see. If I have him on a lead with me at night, the cops never pick me up.'

3

ARISTOCRATIC ANIMALS

The 8th Earl of Bridgwater was a typical eighteenth century aristocratic hedonist. Although Rector of two Wiltshire parishes, he was never there and paid a pittance instead for some drudge of a cleric to do the work for him while he spent the latter part of his life in a Paris mansion entertaining to dinner almost every night not humans but eleven dogs chosen from his collection and elegantly attired, with napkins round their necks. Seated at the head of the table, he would talk to them about the news of the day, while they were served. All were well trained, but should any one of them behave badly, the culprit would be banished to the kitchen, stripped of all finery and clad like a scullion until judged fit to resume dining with the Earl. Both he and his dogs wore shoes and boots of leather, made to measure, changing them daily and never wearing the same pair again during the course of a year. These cosseted creatures would be taken out by Bridgwater in his carriage for rides in the Bois de Boulogne, accompanied by attendants in livery.

* * *

Such infatuation with pets can lead to friction between husband and wife. For example, in 1931, the Duke of Marlborough quitted his ancestral home at Blenheim Palace because he could no longer put up with the way his wife's spaniels were taking over the place. Ignoring his protests, Gladys had ordered carpenters to cut away sections in the walls of the state rooms and install doors that were kept open so that the dogs could run about as they wished. The Great Hall was divided into dog coops that reeked, and as more spaniels were bred, pens were erected in the other rooms so that Gladys could always have them around her. The Duke, who was in his early sixties and whose nickname was 'Sunny', used to swear at the dogs and search for new stains on the carpets to point out to his guests.

* * *

An eccentric peer of the same period was Viscount Tredegar, who had his own menagerie in the park of his castle in Wales and excelled at taming birds. His closest friend was a macaw who was so jealously possessive that she would peck and drive away anyone approaching him when they were together. In his South Street, London, house, there was a cage of monkeys halfway up the stairs. He inherited his love of birds from his mother, whose hobby was making impressive reproductions of birds' nests, and was believed to have made a large model with mud so that she could sit in it herself.

* * *

A peer in more recent times with an unusual taste in pets was the Earl of Cranbrook. He had a passion for bats which he exercised in his bathroom. The *Christian Science Monitor* for January 27, 1967, reported him as saying: 'I keep them for about three months, feed them well, then let them go.' His recipe for an ideal bat-meal was the yolk of a hard-boiled egg, cream cheese and banana in equal portions.

* * *

Though, in common with other rulers, the Maharajah of Junagadh lost his power with the departure of the British from India, he remained a millionaire, enabling him to go on lavishing luxury on his dogs, giving them all their own suites and retainers to minister to their needs and whims. When his favourite bitch, Roshana, wed Bobby, a Labrador, the wedding breakfast alone cost £60,000, and when the pets left their earthly paradise for good, they were taken to marble mausoleums to the music of Chopin's Funeral March.

The governor and reincarnation

On the evening that Sir Robert Grant, Governor of Bombay, died in 1838, a cat was seen to leave Government House near Poona and walk up and down a path as the deceased used to do after sunset. A Hindu sentry noticed this and mentioned it to his fellow soldiers. Full of superstitious awe, they consulted a Brahmin who told them that we all have an essential element, apart from the physical body, that is repeatedly reborn into

31

different bodies before achieving eventual salvation. The Governor's spirit had now entered into a cat. It was difficult to identify a particular one as there were so many looking alike, so it was decided that every cat passing out of the main entrance after dark was to be regarded as the reincarnated Governor and treated with due respect and the appropriate honours.

This decision was accepted without question by the whole guard, and from then onwards for 25 years the sentry at the front door would present arms to any cat passing out after dark. At the end of that time, Sir Thomas Gordon became Governor and in his memoirs he wrote that learning of this custom he took the matter up with the commanding officers of the two infantry regiments providing the sepoy guard on alternate weeks. One, a man of calm judgement, said he would tactfully laugh his native officers out of the superstition, but the other, a rigid disciplinarian, immediately summoned them and ordered that no cat be saluted in future. He warned that anyone disobeying would be court-martialled.

When the first guard by this regiment after the warning returned from the week's duty at Government House, the subahdar in command was questioned. It then came out that his fear of the supernatural was greater than his fear of the stern, uncompromising colonel, and he confessed that to act as ordered would have been against his religious convictions, and having disobeyed, he was prepared to lose rank in the army and his pension. His CO was enraged by such insubordination, placed the man under arrest, and prepared an application for his trial by court martial. The brigadier, however, took a tolerant view of the case, ordered the native officer to be released and quietly advised the colonel to deal more gently and patiently with simple superstitions.

* * *

ARISTOCRATIC ANIMALS

A few years ago, Fleur Cowles asked a number of famous people which animals they would like to be reincarnated as, and why. It was for a book to raise funds for the World Wildlife Fund. Twiggy said she would like to be a gorilla, David Dimbleby a tortoise, Lord Carrington a house martin, and Fleur herself a cheetah.

4

HEROES AND VILLAINS

The Dickin Medal, regarded as the Animal VC, was awarded in April, 1946, to a pedigree pointer bitch, born ten years earlier at the Shanghai Dog Kennels, originally named Shudi, meaning 'peaceful' in Chinese, and later Anglicized to Judy, and bought as the ship's pet of HMS *Gnat*, one of the gunboats patrolling the lower reaches of the Yangtse River against bandits and pirates. Able to hear sounds the human ear could not detect, her warning barks soon proved invaluable.

In June, 1939, half of the crew together with Judy were transferred to a more modern gunboat, HMS *Grasshopper*, based in Singapore. Then when the Japanese invaders reduced that Gibraltar of the East to a raging inferno, the gunboats crowded with refugees made southwards but the *Grasshopper* was sunk by dive-bombers. Judy was missing when the survivors landed on the beach of a small island. The coxswain, sent back to the wreck to see what he could salvage, found Judy trapped under toppled lockers. She soon repaid them for being rescued. They had no fresh water and the situation became desperate, but somehow she seemed to understand what was being sought, kept whining and digging at a certain place in the wet sand, then tugged the Chief Petty Officer towards it, so he lent a hand, and presently clear fresh water surged up.

Five days later, they were rescued and eventually made for Padang in Sumatra where it was believed naval vessels were waiting to convey them to Colombo. The last 170 miles of the journey were on foot through the jungle and took them five weeks. Judy, as in the past, behaved as though they were all her responsibility. She tirelessly went ahead, leading them over firm ground, killing snakes and warning them of other hidden dangers. But when they reached Padang, the last ship had left and soon the Japs arrived and, in due course, the Navy men were imprisoned in barracks near Medan. It was here that Judy met the young RAF technician, Frank Williams, whom she was to regard for the rest of her life as master. Highly intelligent, she rapidly acquired a talent for comprehending any whispered messages from him, such as when she stole for them the fruit which, instead of flowers, were laid on Japanese graves. This improved the watered-down rice which was their only food. Judy herself was not allowed anything to eat by their captors so had to go foraging in the jungle, and she was in constant danger of being hurled into a stew-pot and eaten by them.

Then, one day, Williams noticed that Judy had developed a significant bulge. He and his comrades were astonished, and some joked that she would be giving birth to a litter of baby tigers. However, she produced nine pups, so must have attracted about the only wild dog not killed in the jungle as her mate. This event gave Frank a brainwave. The Commandant of the camp's girl friend had taken a liking to Judy. So one evening when Colonel Banno was alone drinking, Williams risked being executed, knocked on the door of the Jap's hut and entered carrying Kish, the finest of the pups, and set it down on the table in front of Banno, whose hand it proceeded to lick. This was rewarded with uproarious laughter and by acceptance of the puppy as a gift for the lady.

Williams now asked that Judy be added to the list of

official prisoners-of-war which would remove the risk of her being killed, but the Colonel, though sympathetic, refused on the grounds that headquarters would ask questions if an extra number were added to the list and he might find himself in serious trouble.

Frank Williams was quick to suggest a way round this — by adding 'A' to his own number. The Colonel was happily playing with the puppy as though she were his lady love and, caught at the right moment, accepted this way round the problem. He wrote out the necessary chit giving official effect to the change — and next day Judy could be seen bearing a tag prominently inscribed '81A MEDAN'.

Shortly afterwards, unfortunately, a Captain Nissi took over and he forced all the prisoners to work harder. Then he announced that they were all to be shipped to Singapore but he refused to let Frank take Judy with him. The RAF technician, nevertheless, was determined to do so despite the fact that discovery would result in both being executed. He thought out carefully a plan to outwit Nissi. He would bring his pet to the place of embarkation by carrying her hidden in a sack whenever there was any risk of the guards seeing her. So he taught her to leap inside it the moment he clicked his fingers, and when the time of departure came, he fastened Judy to a pole in the main hut in such a way that the slip-knot would give way if she pulled at it. Telling her to 'stay', he went to join the other prisoners preparing to leave, and over his shoulder hung the sack stuffed with a blanket.

Once outside the camp, Frank whistled softly and the clever pointer stole under cover of bushes to the railway and hid under a wagon until her master arrived. Screened by the other men, he removed the blanket and holding out the sack clicked his fingers and Judy jumped in. All went well until they were on board the ancient tramp steamer making for Singapore and it was hit by two torpedoes probably fired in error by a Japanese submarine. Over five hundred of the seven hundred POWs herded in the holds perished. Realising it was impossible for him to force his way with Judy through the wreckage, Frank pushed her through a porthole, telling her to swim for it. Then, with difficulty, he reached the deck and plunged into the sea. Two hours later, in a state of utter exhaustion, he was dragged aboard a Japanese tanker.

Meanwhile, Judy had proved herself a life saving heroine. Paddling resolutely, with head stretched well above the sea, she had helped several of her human friends as each in turn supported himself on her back until a boat rescued him. But far from being rewarded on reaching Singapore, she caught the eye of Captain Nissi who had got there ahead of them and who, furious at her having been smuggled away contrary to his orders, shouted to two soldiers to shoot her. Fortunately, however, Colonel Banno happened to be present and he intervened, saving Judy's life.

A month later, the prisoners were shipped back to Sumatra, then marched through the jungle in torrential rain to Sawaluento to be employed as a railway construction gang under the most horrific conditions. Up to ten men a day died. Judy accompanied Frank Williams as he drove metal spikes with a sledge hammer into the sleepers. Tom Scott, one of the prisoners, has written that she was now thin, half starved, her eyes only softening when Frank touched her or spoke to her, or when she looked up at him. Whenever she found herself too close to one of the guards, her lip curled back in a snarl, and her eyes seemed to glow with almost a red glare. Sometimes, when a guard threatened to retaliate, Frank would click his fingers and Judy would disappear into the jungle. Then the moment he gave a low whistle, she would be back.

Reports were now reaching these railroad slaves that the tide of war had turned against their persecutors, but meanwhile Judy's life was increasingly imperilled – first, when she sprang at a guard beating a prisoner over the head with a stave and the Jap retaliated by firing at the pointer, lacerating her shoulder; and next, when it was discovered that the prisoners had lice, Judy was wrongfully blamed and condemned to be shot. For two days, she outwitted the guards by vanishing into the jungle whenever they came after her. Then it was the Japs who made themselves scarce as Judy led into the camp two soldiers wearing red berets – the spearhead of the Parachute Regiment. The war was over.

It was 1946 and, in the Chinese calendar, the 'Year of the Dog', and it certainly proved to be a fortunate one for Judy. Frank Williams brought her to England with him and after spending the required six months at the Hackbridge Quarantine Kennels where he visited her frequently, Judy reaped a well-deserved harvest of honours. The citation accompanying the Dickin Medal read: 'For magnificent courage and endurance in Japanese prison camps, thus helping to maintain morale among her fellow prisoners and for saving many lives by her intelligence and watchfulness.' She was invited to become the only canine member of the Returned Prisoners of War Association and also barked eloquently at the microphone when interviewed on the BBC's 'In Town Tonight' programme.

Two years later, Frank Williams emigrated to East Africa where Judy spent an enjoyable and eventful life before dying peacefully in 1950. Her master buried her, wrapped in an RAF jacket, in Nachingwea, and erected a marble monument to, as he puts it, 'a gallant old girl, a wonderful dog, which, with wagging tail, gave more affection and companionship than she ever received'.

In 1970, when the members of the Yangtse Gunboatmen's Association met for their first annual reunion, four of them, Vic Oliver, Bill Wilson, George White and Les Searle, who had known Judy and had taken part in some of her experiences, decided to undertake all the work involved in writing her life story, and this was later published in 1973 under the title of *THE JUDY STORY — The Dog with Six Lives.*

Award winners

There were several other awards of the Dickin Medal to animals showing exceptional bravery in dangerous circumstances during the Second World War. Beauty, a wire-haired terrier, and Irma, Rex, Thorn and Jet, all Alsatians, saved hundreds of lives during the Blitz by sniffing out survivors buried under rubble. Irma could tell the difference between live and dead casualties. A bark would mean that she had located a survivor; a wag of her tail, a corpse.

Most celebrated of the mine-detecting canine heroes was Ricky, a scruffy Welsh sheepdog with a winsome nature, who was searching for explosives laid by the Germans on a Dutch canal bank when a mine exploded some feet away, killing an officer and badly wounding Ricky in the face. Despite this injury, he resolutely went on with his task. Lent to the Army for the duration of the war, Ricky returned to his owner when hostilities ceased. The military were reluctant to let him go and tried to buy him offering a large amount, but it was refused.

Another recipient of the ribbon coloured green, brown, and light blue, signifying valour on sea, land, and in the sky, was the Alsatian, Rifleman Khan, who served with the Commandos attacking the Dutch island of Walcheren in 1944. Khan and his handler were pressing on through the gunfire when their craft capsized. The dog managed to gain the beach but Corporal Muldoon, unable to swim, would have drowned had not Khan dived back into the sea, and, avoiding the shells, spotted his master and hauled him to the shore.

Rip, a famished mongrel, was saved from the fate of the half million strays destroyed through their being abandoned owing to call-ups and evacuations. The Poplar ARP wardens gave Rip a home and later elevated him to the position of mascot, which he richly deserved for he began sniffing out those imprisoned in bombed buildings. He saved well over two hundred lives in this way, and was rewarded, too, with the Dickin Medal, which also was awarded to Rob, another mongrel, who jumped by parachute over twenty times with the SAS into North Africa and Italy, then protected them during their perilous engagements.

At the Army War Dog School in Potters Bar, Alsatians during the war were trained for guard and patrol duties, and at sea many ships kept a dog whose astonishingly sharp hearing gave early warning of hostile aircraft in the far distance. The most tragic event affecting the canine race during the Second World War occurred in Russia when it looked as if Moscow would fall to the Germans whose tanks were making relentlessly towards it. To try and halt the advance, hundreds of trained dogs were sent racing across the open ground to hover under the armoured monsters until the primed bombs strapped to the dogs' backs exploded.

* * *

The deeds of police dogs in defying danger receives official commendation through the Action of the Year Award. In 1982, a seven-year-old bitch, Myra, about to retire, was one of the two canines thus honoured. Angela Patmore in her book, *Your Obedient Servant*, reported what Police

Constable Ray Cooper of the Met told her when she interviewed him. He was on duty in the Piccadilly area with
other dog-handlers, as they had been informed that
serious trouble was expected between Chelsea and Leeds
football supporters. This resulted in his finding himself
alone with Myra on the westbound Piccadilly station
platform faced with trying to quell the fighting between
some three hundred Soccer rowdies. Myra split them up
and forced a passage between the brawling opponents.
Most of the Chelsea mob fled. One hundred and fifty-three
of the Leeds faction had retreated to the end of the platform with no ways of escape other than through the
tunnel or along the rails. So Ray Cooper and Myra con-
fronted the breakers of the peace, who charged again and
again, only to be driven back by Myra who kept them
corralled until police reinforcements came and took them
into custody.

'Myra's a very small bitch and not alarming to look at,'
PC Ray Cooper told Angela Patmore, and added that
what Myra lacked in size, she made up for in aggression.

Angela Patmore comments that many dogs in blue are
cast-offs from the public, and that the police like them all
the better on that account. 'They say the backyard
castaway has the best character. He'll do anything for
"dad".'

* * *

In his book, *My Dog Tulip*, J R Ackerley tells of a Collie
of considerable character that took his role as guardian
of the law very seriously at the pub where he lived. At
opening time, he would hang over the first floor balcony
monitoring every customer entering or leaving, then
creep downstairs and lie under the bar until hearing the

call of 'Last orders, please!', he would spring up, put his feet on the counter and keep barking until everyone left.

Court appearance

It is perhaps only natural that members of the legal profession should hope that their pets will be law-abiding, but what steps should be taken if they are not? Lord Eldon was a Scottish judge highly regarded in Edinburgh during the late eighteenth and early nineteenth centuries. A bachelor, he doted as much on cats as his predecessor, Lord Gardenstone, had on pigs, and preferred half-a-dozen of them to keep him company rather than risk having a nagging wife. Nevertheless, there were times when his relations with these feline friends were extremely strained. One day, when studying the evidence in a complicated case, such a cacophonous caterwauling broke out below his study window that he threw it open and in his most magisterial voice ordered the offenders to cease making such a row. But his pets took not the slightest notice, so before resorting to sterner measures, Eldon magnanimously chose to give the cats the full benefit of the law as if they were unruly human beings. He proceeded in his gravest tones to read the Riot Act. The cats, however, caterwauled all the louder. Outraged by such flouting of his authority, the judge seized a pistol and fired it among his tormentors scattering them.

* * *

There have been a number of cases where an eloquent advocate has so moved a jury with his final speech that they have not only found in his client's favour but have awarded damages in excess of the sum expected. In the United States, the owner of a dog sued the man who had killed his pet, and this is the speech that the late Senator Vest of Missouri made to the jury on behalf of his client:

'The best friend a man has in this world may turn against him. His son and daughter whom he has raised with loving care may become ungrateful . . . The people who are prone to fall to their knees to do us honour when success is with us may be the first to throw the stone of malice when failure settles its cloud upon our heads. The only unselfish friend a man may have in this world is his dog . . . He will sleep on the cold ground when the wintry wind blows and the snow drives fiercely, if only he may be near his master's side. He will kiss the hand that has no food to offer. He will lick the wounds and sores that come in encounters with the roughness of the world . . . and when the last scene of all comes . . . there by the graveside will the noble dog be found, his head between his paws and his eyes sad, but open in alert watchfulness, faithful and true even to death.'

The jury were so moved after listening to this that they awarded $500 as damages instead of the $200 originally claimed and asked the judge if the defendant could not be imprisoned as well.

Senator Vest's references to the devotion displayed by dogs towards their owners are well supported by cases such as that of Hachiko, the Akita, who used to accompany his master, a Tokyo University Professor, every morning to Shibuya Station, and then return at 5 p.m. to await the train bringing him back. But one afternoon in 1925 Hachiko waited in vain, for the Professor had died from a heart attack while lecturing. Nevertheless, the dog went on going daily to the station without fail at the same time until he died ten years later. This created such an impression among the Japanese that a

...tue of the 'Loyal Dog' now marks the place where he

...r dog spent more than fifteen barren years in ...isits to the same spot in the Italian village of Bo... San Lorenzo where master used to get down from the bus bringing him home from work.

In 1943 the mongrel Fido's owner had not returned, for he had been killed in a bombing raid on Florence. Eventually, the villagers decided to commemorate the dog's faithfulness by presenting him with a gold medal. A crowd gathered to witness the ceremony, then, just as the Mayor was on the point of fastening the medal to Fido's collar, the recipient darted off – must not be late for that bus in case master turned up at last.

5

WILD AND WONDERFUL

...title of Baroness Elizabeth Becker's fascinating account of the many diverse pets that have given her immense pleasure. The first was a ferret which as a child she would bathe every Sunday evening, and though he protested while spluttering in the soapy water, afterwards he would puff out his immaculate tail with pride uttering 'high-pitched little noises of pure pleasure'. Next, she cherished Sally, a dilapidated hen, which enjoyed a long life and sat on a just-born, abandoned black kitten young Elizabeth had saved, then brought up as if it were its own chick, thereby initiating her experiments of raising together animals that are not only dissimilar but usually believed to be enemies.

When aged fourteen, Elizabeth became the owner of a hooded rat, a species which she describes as 'the most charming, faithful, affectionate and intelligent of creatures'. Angelica resided and was taken out and about in a cage cosily enveloped in red flannel with her name embroidered large on it. Following her marriage, the Baroness acquired another tiny hooded white rat, named Rattle Pratt, that could not have been more docile and resided in a tin-lined hamster cage on the landing. He was happiest of all when nestling on the Beckers' laps, in their bed or pockets, and accompanied them abroad in a tennis ball box, passing the day snoozing concealed in drawer or cupboard. When dining in restaurants Baroness would drop pieces of hard-boiled eggs, and a and other titbits and pop them into her handbag. comments that anybody noticing this might regarded her as an eccentric Englishwoman or a sufferer from night starvation. But all that concerned her was the fact that Rattle Pratt, eagerly awaiting her return, would dash out to grab in his tiny pink paws what she had collected for him.

Tiring of town life, the Beckers went to live in the country. Itsy, who became fast friends with Binnie licked her and Itsy drank ... latest pet; Norah proved that the phrase 'to eat like a fighter' completely untrue for she ate daintily and tidily. Baroness describes her as 'an absolute vacuum cleaner who 'with her round cushion of a nose exactly angled' left behind not a speck upon the carpet. Unfortunately, she died young through overdoing bathing with the dogs in the stream and catching pneumonia.

When Rattle, too, passed away, he was replaced by another white rat named Infestus because Baron Becker complained to his wife: 'Now you are going to infest us with white rats again.' Then, after purchasing a bush baby called Fricky, the Baroness learnt that being a primate he must never be left alone with Infestus, a rodent, or else there might be a disastrous duel. All the same, despite such expert advice, she took a more optimistic outlook, for her son's cat that had always hunted rodents had never even attempted to attack Infestus, who was a big buck rat in his prime but a third of the size of the bush baby. So she tried an experiment and brought them together in her bedroom with husband Peter present in case of trouble. When Fricky spotted Infestus on top of a chest of drawers, he was up in a flash grasping the other by the ear. But the rat nonchalantly freed himself and made for the edge, intent on making his way down so as to find the Baroness.

Fricky stared uncertainly at the plump posterior facing him, advanced warily, then sniffed exploratively. The Baroness was overcome with apprehension. Would her experiment fail? Fortunately, it succeeded, for the bush baby turned aside and, jumping down, careered round the room. With immense relief, she knew that these two pets would tolerate each other and that she need not keep them apart.

Infestus resided in a cardboard box with an opening to it kept in a corner of the Baroness's bathroom, and inside which he stored his eatables. Following the bush baby's peaceful introduction to him, Fricky, also, was accommodated there. The state of amicable coexistence established between them facilitated transport of the pets between the country and London. One day when the Baroness had to be away from home longer than usual, she made a number of holes in a rectangular beauty case, cushioned it with a woolly, and, while Fricky was asleep, placed him inside. Then, she risked laying dozing Infestus above the other before carefully replacing the lid – and hoped for the best.

Much later that day when in town, the Baroness apprehensively took a quick look into the box and was amazed to find Infestus embraced in Fricky's arms and his head nestling under the bush baby's comfortable chin. What a splendid hot water bottle the white rat made, thought his owner, and after this the pair were conveyed everywhere in the beauty case.

Such a successful experiment supports the views of Dr Michael W. Fox of the Wild Canid Research Center of St Louis in the United States. In his book, *Understanding Your Cat*, he writes about how a fiifteen-year-old cat had brought an infant chipmunk home to play with and still played with it, which Dr Fox regarded as strong evidence for one of his main beliefs. 'Pets need pets, and provided no one is frustrated and deprived of security, food and affection, prey and predator, mouse and lion, can and will, live peacefully together.'

John Aspinall

John Aspinall is famed for his love of animals — and gambling. He was first attracted to gorillas through secret visits by himself to the London Zoo where he gained infinite pleasure watching the famed silverback male, Guy, whose keeper permitted Aspinall to feed with fine fruit and chat to the noble creature inside his enclosure. As a result of this experience, John bought a gorilla which had been ill-treated and with his mother-in-law's help — such as allowing him to sleep in her bed — did all he could to rehabilitate Kivu but the animal died within a year. Next he acquired a male and a female, Gugis and Shamba, from whom he gained much of his considerable insight into the character and customs of gorillas. This led to his assembling as well at Howletts bears, cheetahs and tigers, based on the principle of no restrictions on their activities and the encouragement of amicable relations between all kinds.

Bought from a pet shop when only nine weeks old, Tara the tigress had been described by John Aspinall as a mind-opener for him. They raised her on the bottle and she slept in his bed for the first year and a half. He says that she was so reliable and affectionate that he assumed at first that she was an exceptional animal, but experience later taught him that her virtues were common to her race. He concluded that to some degree he must have been affected by the long-standing prejudice against tigers because he was surprised that she never showed any inclination to injure others or sulked if corrected. Neither did the progressive change from a milk to a meat diet, or the reaching of puberty, make her aggressive. He claims that his extensive experience of many tigers has proved that 'even extreme hunger fails to dispel their trust and love of man once given and once earned'.

John Aspinall has also disputed the advice that to approach a tigress when with her cubs is to invite attack. He entered Tara's den soon after she had given birth to her first litter and was welcomed with purrs. When a cub came towards him, he took it into his arms. Far from reacting violently, Tara immediately picked up the other one in her jaws and deposited it in his lap for admiration.

Aspinall's concern for the welfare of his animal friends is well-known. A gorilla needing a hernia operation was taken by car for surgery to a top clinic in Harley Street. On another occasion, decorators employed to do some wallpapering upstairs in his mother-in-law's cottage in the grounds at Howletts were asked by her to be as quiet as possible so as not to disturb two sleeping gorillas. The men no doubt thought the animals were resting in a cage outside. Then, as work was started, two huge heads reared up from under blankets on a bed protesting vociferously at the intrusion. Unnerved, the decorators fled, never to return.

Another contretemps arose when a coalman called who was unaware of the fact that Zemo, an amiable tiger, was taking a nap close by beneath a laurel bush and that the animal's pastime was to attack empty sacks and rend them to bits. He was usually allotted one or two every day to amuse him. When the man took a breather after tipping out the coke from a number of sacks, he was horrified to spot a large tiger nearby about to leap. He shrieked in terror as Zemo charged at the sacks with chilling roars. The coalman was found later quaking on his knees as he prayed aloud.

The parrot jungle

In 1936, Austrian-born Franz Scherr and his wife, Louise, started a 40-acre sanctuary for uncaged tropical birds at Miami to which in ensuing years visitors to Florida were to flock. Louise was originally sceptical that the exotic birds, which numbered more than a thousand, would remain there, but they did. In the case of the parrots, he took precautions by clipping their wings first, and was gratified to find that by the time fresh feathers had sprouted they regarded the sanctuary as their Eden where they lived on plenty of peanuts, sunflower seeds, pecans and fruit.

The Scherrs found that the blue and gold macaws were more perceptive and responsive than the others. They were quick at learning to perform tricks and revelled in being rewarded with applause and nuts. For a whole year one of them called Pop kept a sharp eye on Susie, a capuchin, ringtailed monkey, as she went through the motions of an act showing off her skill. Stretching an arm through the bars of her cage, Susie would seize a stick, using it to pull towards her a longer one with which she dragged a cane inside. With this she would draw a set of three canisters towards her, take out of the smallest one a glass jar, unscrew its top and gleefully seize a peanut.

Pop made up his mind that he, too, could do this, so for a year he practised with the cans thrown down by tourists and eventually performed as faultlessly as Susie.

The parrots cared for by the Scherrs were astonishingly gifted and not only responded to their names but waved flags, rode bicycles, played cards, roller-skated, and counted.

Dr Schweitzer at Lambarene

Writing in *Animal Life* for November, 1962, Guy

Barthélemy described a visit to Dr Albert Schweitzer and his animals at Lambarene in the heart of equatorial Africa. Perched all along the overhead pipes conveying drinking water were pelicans and other birds, recovering from injuries which the good doctor had treated. 'At one time,' he would tell visitors laughingly, 'you couldn't have come anywhere near my room without running a considerable risk. A pelican, who had appointed himself my guardian, took up a permanent post on the front of the roof of the gallery and administered magnificent blows with his beak on the heads of all intruders. When I went up river to visit patients, he placed himself in the bows of the canoe and there he stayed.'

Parrots boarded at Lambarene paid for their keep in a practical way. Schweitzer revealed that he no longer needed to watch his workmen. The moment they slackened and started chattering they heard him shouting, 'Get on with your work!' and started exerting themselves in earnest, while in a nearby palm tree a parrot chortled triumphantly to himself for he had copied their employer's voice admirably.

The Gaboon breed of bird were also superb mimics. One of these was the pet of a young doctor at the hospital and when he came on duty in the morning, it would approach him, coughing, groaning and so on in such easily identifiable tones that he had no trouble in linking them individually with the white patients in their ward which the bird had gone round earlier on. To the amazement of the bed-ridden, the doctor was thus so well briefed that he was able to say to each in turn, 'You've been coughing a lot all night?' or 'What's wrong with your liver?' As a result of this, the doctor was credited with second sight.

Barthélemy describes Dr Schweitzer's office as more like a zoo than a place of work. There were little gazelles and antelopes lying close and snug on a comfortable straw mattress in one corner. Among them was an old blind antelope and it needed infinite patience and loving care to pilot her back after her daily constitutional. The baby gazelles and antelopes, before moving into an enclosure facing Schweitzer's room, enjoyed being with him in his office despite its narrowness. When at nightfall he sat at the piano to play a Bach prelude, they would arrange themselves by his feet. Occasionally, his performance would be disturbed by one of the small creatures daring to nibble at pages from a book he was writing which he had forgotten to put out of reach. On account of the appetite antelopes have for manuscripts, he had to fasten together the sheets of paper and suspend them from the ceiling.

'I'm going to introduce you to the prettiest little pig in the world,' Dr Schweitzer would announce to people being shown round, then summon in kindly tones: 'Isabelle! Isabelle!' and a huge, reddish brown hippopotamus-like animal weighing about 3 cwt would make towards them, amiably greeting the stranger by rubbing off the mud with which she was coated on to his white trousers, then rolling over in the hope that the Doctor would scratch her stomach with his boots. 'Isn't Isabelle sweet?' he would say, then lowering his voice add: 'You mustn't say no – it wouldn't be polite. I brought her up myself on the bottle after she was brought to me out of the jungle by a native hunter who had killed her mother.'

'Ibamba'

In 1926-9, Wynant Davis Hubbard bought land in Northern Rhodesia and started a research station to study wild animals. He relates his experiences in an excellent book, *Ibamba*, which convinced him that if one could bring them up in human company from when they were babies none would later revert to a savage state. He lists 'infant wart hogs, leopards, elephants, antelopes, bush cats, cheetahs, rhinoceroses, buffaloes, zebras, owls, cranes, lions, hornbills, doves, hedgehogs, and turtles and tortoises' as passing through his hands and leaving him with the conclusion that environment and upbringing determine the development of a baby animal and 'not inherited emotional or mental characteristics'.

Joy Adamson in *Born Free* about Elsa, reared by her from infancy with human beings, describes how, instead of reverting, the lioness had to be prepared and instructed to enable her to cope with what should have been her natural life on the open veldt.

Lions were Mr Hubbard's favourite animals and one day there was brought to him in a cage the most wretched specimen of a baby one that he had ever seen. They named her Paddy on account of her huge flapping front paws that looked larger than normal because the rest of her was skin and bones. It took weeks of intensive nursing to save her life. When she was introduced to the other animals they kept Paddy sniffed all over each one to be certain she would recognize them again before moving away. No one had disclosed to her that young lionesses ought to be at daggers drawn with Fwifwi the little antelope, Mr Thomas the civet cat, the crested cranes and the dogs. Ignorant of her forbears' animosities, Paddy made them all her pals.

Mr Thomas had been the Hubbards' first civet cat pet and had proved wrong the belief that they were untameable. Once he was old enough to make his way about the house without help, they left a large enamel basin full of water on the verandah so that he and Fwifwi could refresh themselves with a drink whenever they wished. Mr Thomas, however, assumed it to be a pets' WC and used it as such — never did he make a mess indoors.

Paddy developed into a sturdy, lively teenager of a

lioness who would enjoy herself rolling and wrestling on the floor with her human master. She would bite and claw his shirt to shreds, but, except by accident, she never so much as scratched him. Should this happen and he pointed at the injury, Paddy would run her nose over the droplet of blood and express her sorrow by licking it away, gently accompanied by moans and groans. Paddy was devoted to Buncher, the Hubbards' small daughter, and if she cried the lioness was instantly concerned and if she thought they were the cause through refusing her something, Paddy would become Buncher's champion and snarl at them.

Mr Hubbard has some interesting observations to make regarding the reactions of animals to perfume. The civet cat's favourite was pure household ammonia on a bit of cotton, against which he would rub one cheek and then the other until it was pressed flat to the floor and all the ammonia extracted. Mr Hubbard says that keepers of lions in the world's zoos would no doubt be astonished and upset to learn that it was possible to turn the biggest, most imposing and haughty lion into a maudlin, foolish beast by offering it a whiff of perfume.

The Hubbards visited a zoo and obtained permission to go behind the rail which separated the cages from the viewing area. They pushed a piece of cotton-wool impregnated with catnip oil through the bars before the nose of an ancient and morose lion who perked up immediately, but the scent which had the most effect upon him was that of the cheapest and strongest they had bought. When cotton-wool soaked with this was thrown before him and he picked it up, the effect upon his behaviour was startling. Crying and gurgling in ecstasy, he sank on to the floor, rubbing his cheeks with it and pushing it up his nostrils. So entranced did he become that he took no notice when they reached between the bars to touch him. Other lions on whom they experimented with perfume behaved in precisely the same

way. Lionesses, leopards and tigers did not react with
such rapture.

Rufus the rhino

In her book, *Rufus the Rhino*, Yuilleen Kearney, wife of
an Assistant Warden of the Tsavo National Park in
Kenya, tells the story of the baby rhino, 18 inches high
and weighing only 50 lbs, lost by his mother, who arrived
in their cook's hut almost dying and who by feeding on
lactogen milk they succeeded in transforming into a
happy, healthy animal who tailed Yuilleen everywhere
and enjoyed most of all being brushed every day with her
best hairbrush. He had for companions her other pets –
three baby mongooses and Felix, a melanic civet cat. For
Rufus's first birthday she baked a large cake made of his
favourite food, maize meal, sprinkling it with white flour
to resemble icing. When the young rhino saw it, he
rushed up panting with such pleasure that he puffed most
of the 'icing' over husband Dennis. Ready with her
camera, Yuilleen snapped him offering Rufus a slice of
the cake, but before she could take another picture he had
consumed the rest of the cake except for the candles.

Rufus's front horn was now some 2 inches long and had
some way to go before it approached the maximum length
of 3 feet as an adult. Nevertheless, he was proud of this
beginning and busied himself burnishing it in the red
earth. Having outgrown the stable shared with two
buffaloes he was allotted sleeping quarters in a larger one
but had grown so fond of Yuilleen that he tried all manner
of tricks to avoid being taken away by the herdsman at
bedtime. Jealous of strangers, he attacked any approaching her and once they had fled would settle down beside
her grunting with satisfaction that he had her company

exclusively to himself once more. If she and her husband were absent for any length of time, Rufus began to blubber the moment the Land Rover left and sulked until she returned.

Rufus seemed quite unaware of the growing havoc his bulk and vigour caused to furniture as he amused himself in their rooms, so a large pen was erected to accommodate him during the day and here he was introduced to Aruba, a tame and frolicsome young elephant who revelled in Rufus's company, looping her trunk round his barrel-like back and about his face whilst uttering amorous rumbling sounds. She became so possessive that the two buffaloes, Susannah and Buster, who shared the pen with them, were kept at a distance from Rufus. The pair always fed, side by side, and when Rufus took a siesta, Aruba would act sentry by standing over his recumbent form with legs straddled and thrashing the air threateningly as a 'keep well away' signal.

Rufus thoroughly enjoyed being fussed over by Aruba, but the one he adored was his human mistress and her daily visit did not satisfy him. Once when on the way back with the other four animals and their keeper from a long walk, he stole away while pretending to graze in the bush and the distraught herdsman searched in every direction for him before at long last making for the house to report the disaster, only to discover the fugitive resting in his favourite spot on Yuilleen's verandah.

The second time Rufus escaped from his keeper, instead of stealing away through the bush, he galloped off like a wild rhino taking the shortest route, stopped before the verandah, walked resolutely up the steps, sat down beside Yuilleen in her deck-chair, asked to be given a good scratch and many lumps of sugar and began a lengthy conversation in rhino language, interspersed with a great deal of petting and patting from her. Satisfied at last, Rufus fell asleep.

Rufus's third such adventure had a less happy ending.

WILD AND WONDERFUL

The Kearneys, on returning from a day's visit to Mombassa, found their home looking as if it had been attacked by bandits. The rhino, unable to find Yuilleen, had ransacked every room, opening all the cupboards and throwing about their contents.

Soon after this, Dennis was transferred to Nairobi Game Park. Rufus had now reached adulthood and the time had come for parting. Yuilleen Kearney writes that she felt like a Judas as she left Rufus. 'He put up his little face and I kissed it.'

Rascal the racoon

Rascal, the story of Sterling North's pet racoon, won for him a Dutton Animal Book Award. His childhood home was a house on the shores of Lake Kushkonong in Wisconsin. His mother died young and his father believed in letting his son grow up as fancy took him. He wandered and acquired pets – a St Bernard and Poe-the-Crow who lived in the belfry of the church and shouted the only phrase he knew – 'What fun! What fun!' – as solemn parishioners attended church services, weddings and funerals. Attracted by all shining objects, he stole and hoarded brass door-knobs, glass marbles, coins, and a diamond ring.

Sterling's other pets were woodchicks and skunks, and, finally, Rascal the racoon, an endearing furry creature with two big black patches over its eyes, a lively inquisitive nature and clean habits. With Rascal as boon companion, the boy explored, swam, and fished for a whole year, the two of them learning daily from each other. Rascal was fed with the family, and like all racoons washed his food before eating it, so when presented with his first lump of sugar, after feeling and sniffing this

59

mysterious object, he swished it to and fro in his bowl of milk and was astonished when it melted and vanished. He inspected the bottom of the bowl to see if he had dropped it, then peered into the palms of both hands. Lastly, he stared at Sterling and shrilled in racoon language: 'Who has stolen my sugar lump?'

Sterling North wrote in a later book, *The Racoons in My Life*, that they were among the most articulate of all wild animals, uttering thirteen or fourteen calls and many nuances of each. They were 'tender little tremolos of various pitches which are almost songs, many meaningful notes of warning'. Rascal himself loved music and had favourite records which Sterling would play for him on a wind-up Victrola and which even included Wagnerian sopranos.

When Rascal was one year old and began to react to the love calls of a female racoon from the woods, the boy and his father decided to put the pet's natural instincts before their personal pleasure. So Sterling placed Rascal in his customary position in the bows of the boat, paddled it towards the woods and, saying farewell, set him ashore.

Mister B

Irving Petite owned property in Washington State where he felled timber, and when a she-bear who had settled there went off elsewhere, she abandoned an unruly cub which Petite found and adopted. In his book, *Mister B*, he tells what then happened. Brother Paul disapproved, calling the cub 'a real delinquent type', and put him out of the house. The cub climbed a little tree to get out of reach and sat there, snarling and shooting his evictor angry looks. But, says Petite, Mister B could behave quite properly for those who appreciated his qualities. When a cousin filmed him taking exercise and at play, aware of being the centre of attraction, he performed like a gifted Hollywood star. What he needed to keep him happy was to find a substitute for the warm comfort of a mother's body — as a rule Petite's — and would then grasp, chat to, and rub his nose against it. He had the most demonstrative lips and, mounting a leg or a lap, would start nuzzling any part of the upper body he fancied. As he did this, he would mutter 'mmmmm-mmmmm-mmm-mmmm', shutting his eyes and holding on with his nails.

When dislodged, offended Mister B, taking a firm grip with his claws, would swiftly bite the skin he had been massaging with his snout as he protested as well with screams. Subsequently, the cub's yearning for physical contact spread to his attempting to climb up and nuzzle Bill, Petite's partner, their car, some calves and work-horses, as well as a puppy half his size. Most reacted furiously to this, and as a result the puppy grew up with what Petite describes as a 's-t-r-e-t-c-h-e-d' stomach.

Once Mister B was sufficiently strong and self-reliant, Petite decided that it would be best for him if he could return to his mother, so they searched the mountain and eventually found clear tracks of her presence. There they left the cub and for the next two days kept away before stealing back, only to hear the animal shrieking from the hillside beyond where he had been deposited. Bill went off to look for him and late that night reached home carrying their protégé whom he had at last retrieved from the branches of a fir tree.

Once Mister B had fed to repletion, he got into a chair and curling himself up securely fell fast asleep. From time to time, his fur shuddered indicating that he was reliving in nightmares what he had been suffering away from his human friends. Nevertheless, believing it to be for the cub's own good, a week later they again left him near where his mother must be. That night it rained continuously and in the morning when the two men were at the saw mill who should stumble towards them but 'a pitiable dwarf'. Hoping to be a third time lucky, they tried again one evening, but at 2.30 a.m., soaking wet from having fallen in the creek on the way back, he was clawing at their bedroom window and squalling for admittance.

Petite and Bill nevertheless felt that Mister B was getting too big to live in the house all the time, so they prepared a nearby cave for him to sleep in and hoped that one day he might prefer the woods altogether. But the price of freedom cost him his life. One day he did not return from the woods and there were signs that a hunter had slain him and had taken away his body.

'My kingdom for a donkey'

Doris Rybot's favourite toy as a child was an 8 inch tall donkey and ever afterwards she longed to own a real one, so when grown up she bought a country cottage with two small fields by it. Her brother-in-law suggested keeping a donkey there, so she promptly acquired one. In her book, *My Kingdom for a Donkey*, she describes life with Dorcas in an engaging fashion. The new pet kept to the grass for the first day then, attracted by the delights of the vegetable garden, stripped the raspberry canes of all their leaves, topped the artichokes and devoured all she fancied, and then turned her attention to the rest of the garden, denuding the carefully nursed for years bamboo, pruning ruthlessly the jasmine on the west wall, gorging on the leaves of the bay tree, and standing on her hind legs to get at the most delicate shoots of the privet hedge. At least, she turned up her nose at the honeysuckle and the wisteria. Later, they were to find that she had a passion for sweet peas. Doris Rybot understood now why Dorcas's former owner had never referred to her by name, calling her instead 'That *ruddy* donkey!'

Donkeys do not graze but browse and Dorcas's likings out in the fields were as fitful as a goat's — heads of flowering grasses and reeds, thistles, even sometimes a stinging nettle, were her idea of a sort of appetizer. When she discovered infant elm trees in the hedgerows, Dorcas swiftly stripped them of all their leaves. As a rule, however, she preferred a little at a time. A good mixed diet was her aim. After three mouthfuls of peas in their pods, a brace of banana skins and the peel off an orange, she was satisfied and wanted no more. But for lumps of sugar she was a glutton.

Dorcas was a strict vegetarian. Even sugar proffered by a hand that had touched meat would be spurned with disgust, and so, too, would bread that had been near it.

Doris Rybot has some fascinating observations to make about the donkey's vocal range. Her imploring 'hee-haw', made with sides heaving in and out and every noisy breath sounding as if rent from her, was only uttered when she was about to be left alone. It was 'the bagpipes of despair'. On seeing a stranger, she often gave a terrific snort like the trumpeting of a small elephant.

The eerie, jarring bray of the ass has often been the subject of comment. In antiquity, the citizens of Lycopolis banned the blowing of trumpets at public celebrations on account of the similarity. Wordsworth in his poem, *Peter Bell*, referring to the faithful ass mentions 'the hard dry seesaw of his horrible bray', while Jonathan Swift calls the ass 'the nightingale of brutes'.

According to folklore, an ass can only bray, if he lifts his tail. Albert Magnus in *Of the Wonders of the World* (1553) claimed: 'If a stone be bound to the tail of an Ass, he will not bray nor roar.' Doris Rybot points out that when Dorcas was in a wild and wicked mood, galloping free, she might raise her tail to shout, but only then. It hung as limp as a rope when she was complaining.

On several occasions, Dorcas proved herself very bright mentally. Once she got on the opposite side of a chain-link fence from her mistress, whose dog automatically followed. But Dorcas spun round and trotted back to the opening where she had strayed and rejoined Doris on the right side. It is rare for an animal to act so sensibly in such circumstances.

In bed with an elephant

In their book, *Elephant in the Living Room*, Earl and Liz Hammond told the story of Mignon, the baby elephant, who through their loving care grew up to be twice the size of most Indian elephants of her age. She lived with them first in New Jersey and then on their working farm in Pennsylvania where, together with Sasha the bear and other animals they assembled, she was hired out for appearances in movies, TV commercials, and educational programmes – and where a lion actually shared a bed with the elephant.

Mignon was only two months old and the size of a large skinny greyhound when the Hammonds bought her from a Florida animal importer in 1972. They describe her as being 'like a wet noodle with no strength at all'. Food is all important for bringing up such infants. Their mothers' milk is a hundred times richer in albumen than cow's milk which used to make it immensely hazardous to raise them in captivity. A King of Burma once befriended a sacred semi-albino orphaned elephant and recruited relay teams of 24 wet nurses to suckle it for 5 years. The Hammonds fed Mignon on a mixture of three cans of high fat evaporated milk, plus liquid calcium, vitamin supplement and water in a half-gallon bottle. When on a June afternoon Earl first carried Mignon into the living-room of the New Jersey farmhouse, then their home, he was creating a precedent. Never before in that part of the world had anyone attempted to bring up an elephant as one of the family.

They knew nothing about how to house train a baby elephant. An expert friend of theirs declared it to be impossible because these animals lacked the muscular control needed but Liz, who had succeeded in teaching horses to hold back their water while on the stage, believed she could do the same with an elephant. By that evening, Liz's assurance had been undermined. It was as if a mighty river was overflowing its banks at short intervals.

The Hammonds had arranged for Mignon to sleep in the living-room, but hardly had they closed their bedroom door than there came a pitiful cry from her. Liz dashed back and found their new pet terrified at finding herself alone, so they brought in their blankets and settled themselves on the sofa, hoping that their presence would calm her down. But they had little rest for they were regularly awakened by baby's torrential urinating. Next morning, Liz decided that a large bucket was essential, but the problem was how to get it beneath Mignon in time. The solution seemed to be to have her lying on a plastic mat next to them in the bedroom. Like that every time, she started scrambling to her feet, the movement would rouse Liz who would then jump up and place the bucket at the ready.

Liz's next achievement was to train Mignon to rattle the handle of the bucket when she needed to relieve herself and also to wait some seconds to give Liz time to get up. If the rattling did not rouse Liz, Mignon would nudge her with the feeding bottle. Then one night when 'mother's' sleep was particularly profound, 'baby' gave her a black eye with the bottle. Liz shrieked and jumped up, scaring Mignon who ran away and tried ineffectually to hide herself in a corner of the room. This cured her from taking violent action. Instead, when she wanted to wake Liz, she would hover over her gently swinging the feeding bottle until the movement woke her.

One day Mignon attempted to achieve more than she was capable of doing. While Liz was busy in the kitchen, the elephant picked up the bucket with her trunk and placed it in position under her. Then she took a step backwards and trod on the container, flattening it. She stared in puzzlement at the fast growing pool around her. The noise of the bucket being smashed brought Liz hurrying into the room and she could tell from the expression on Mignon's face that baby could not fathom what had gone wrong.

Liz enjoyed the experience of teaching Mignon to go up and down the steps when she took her out for a first airing. She halted at the top and looked questioningly at Liz who signalled that she must find out for herself how to descend the steps, and held a bottle full of milk temptingly before her. Mignon edged forwards and then backwards. At last, she sank down on to her bottom and began to lie on her side. Liz took hold of her front legs and pulled them over the edge of the step. Mignon wriggled around on her rear, while Liz positioned herself two steps below. Then Mignon slowly moved her posterior over the edge and began bumping her way down to the ground. Liz watched, shaking with laughter, then she rewarded Mignon with many congratulatory hugs and a good swig.

On returning, Mignon tried hopping up but failed, so Liz from behind, exerting all the pressure she could, piloted her upwards. At last, despite some slipping, they reached the top. The elephant drew a deep audible breath of relief and to soothe her was given Liz's thumb to suck.

The Hammonds were amused when Mignon started imitating them by sitting in the rocking-chair to watch TV and then switching it off if the programme bored her.

Soon they took her out with them shopping in their Volkswagen. Mignon was so well-behaved that she was allowed inside the supermarket and they were asked if she were a dog wearing an elephant suit. On visits to Kansas City they dined in Max's Restaurant where the owner served her with a special king-sized salad which she ate with delicate elegance. Later in New York, they promenaded with her along Fifth Avenue.

At the end of six weeks, the Hammonds thought it safe to leave Mignon on her own so that they could have a break. A couple were engaged to baby sit one evening and carefully coached in their duties. On returning later, Liz and Earl were horrified to hear Mignon trumpeting for help as they approached. Her minders had pushed her out into the tiny hallway for obstructing their view when they watched TV.

Mignon was distraught and her sides were caving in through dehydration caused when a baby elephant has a bad fright. She started having convulsions. The vet the Hammonds summoned explained that once that happened death invariably followed. He gave her injections and she collapsed on to the Hammonds' bed and fell fast asleep. For almost a week, Liz stayed by the patient's side nursing and comforting her until, to their joy, Mignon began recovering and rose to her feet. Soon husband and wife thought it right that they should be able to sleep together again in their bed and that Mignon should return to the plastic mat, but she refused to do this and kept climbing in and lying next to them. So Earl got up and found an old mattress for her to rest on, but she did not approve of it and went on disturbing them. Every time this occurred, Liz would take her wearily back to the mattress. It looked as though there would be no sleep for them that night. Then Liz had an idea and added sheets and a pillow to Mignon's couch to make it more like their own and at last she settled down.

Liz reveals that she and Earl could not make love without Mignon's sharp hearing detecting this. Jealously disapproving, she would scramble to her feet and, hurrying over, loop her trunk round Liz and attempt to drag her off the bed.

6

POETIC PETS

Byron's favourite dog, a Newfoundland named Boatswain, died of rabies in the poet's arms, aged only five, in
the November before his master's coming of age party and
was buried in the vault of the monk's altar in the garden
of Newstead Abbey, the ancestral home. The inscription
on the tomb composed by Byron describes the dog as one
who 'possessed beauty without vanity, strength without
insolence, courage without ferocity, and all the virtues of
man without vices . . . praise which would be unmeaning
flattery if inscribed over human ashes but is a just tribute
to the Memory of Boatswain, a dog . . .'

A stranger pet was the bear Byron kept with him at
university. Then later, when living with his mistress in
the Ravenna *palazzo* of her husband, one of the richest
men in Italy, Byron surrounded himself with all the
animals and birds he loved. Shelley wrote in a letter
during a visit there: 'Lord Byron's establishment consists,
besides servants, of ten horses, eight enormous dogs,
three monkeys, five rats, an eagle, a crow, and a falcon;
and all these, except the horses, walk about the house,
which every now and then resounds with their unarbi-
trated quarrels as if they were the masters of it . . . After
I have sealed my letter, I find that my enumeration of the
animals in this Circean Palace was defective, and that in

a material point. I have just met on the grand staircase five peacocks, two guinea hens, and an Egyptian crane. I wonder who all these animals were before they changed into these shapes?'

D'Annunzio's goldfish, Adolphus

Italian poets, too, have kept pets. Dante had a favourite cat that liked to sit next to him with a lighted candle between its feet. Gabriele d'Annunzio, when staying in an hotel, took a fancy to a goldfish in a bowl, which he would watch swimming around, talk to it and feed. He named it Adolphus and after leaving still remained so fond of it that he would send regular telegrams to the management enquiring: 'How is my beloved Adolphus?'

In due course, the goldfish died and was thrown out with the rubbish. Soon after this, d'Annunzio telegraphed: 'Feel Adolphus is ill.' The maître d'hôtel replied: 'Adolphus died last night.' To which the poet cabled back: 'Bury him in the garden in a proper grave.' The recipient selected a sardine, covered it with silver paper, and interred it in the garden, marking the spot with a wooden cross bearing the inscription in Italian: 'HERE LIES ADOLPHUS.' When d'Annunzio returned, he laid a sheaf of flowers on the grave and, kneeling, wept over it.

Another Italian poet, Petrarch, was so attached to his cat that when it died he had it embalmed and kept this in a niche in his apartment.

The Methuselah Mouse

One of my best friends is Henry Fearon, poet, naturalist and authority on the countryside. Every week for nearly a quarter of a century his followers would set out on the walks he described so lucidly in the London *Evening News*, writing under the pen-name of 'Fieldfare'. In his home, I have met some of the most appealing of cats and, without exaggeration, there is no gift the children of his neighbourhood appreciate more than a Fearon kitten. The first small pet they had at Craigavad was Methuselah, a white mouse, which when it reached them from Devon was three weeks old, scarcely more than an inch in length, but already with tail and whiskers, of glossy texture, pink-eyed, and snowy white. They accommodated him upon a narrow shelf behind the garage doors.

Relating the story of Methuselah Mouse in his book, *A Lake With Many Fishes*, Henry claims that 'few mousely hearts have beaten more nobly than Methuselah's' and reacted 'with a greater vigour to the dangers and the tribulations of the World of Mice'. He faced many dangers, for the cats of the Fearon household 'do not take kindly to a gentlemanly mouse, and many were the times when his pink eyes viewed the green and yellow ones of our prize mouser less than half an inch away. There was, indeed, a sheet of glass between them; but how was our Methuselah to know with any certainty that his safety lay behind this thin transparency? He showed no fear at all of any of the cats; and as we watched this unawareness in his character – his unawareness of the *danger* of the cats – we liked to believe that this was due to his unfailing trust in us . . .'

However, Henry admits that this might be but fancy, for years of watching Methuselah moving in the safety of his house upon the shelf, as well as his descendants, field mice, harvest mice and shrews, have convinced the Fearons that these tiny creatures have no inherent fear of the cat. It was only when caught that they recognised the cat for their enemy. Henry regards the theory that the smell of one is sufficient to keep the mice away as a complete fallacy. 'In the long run, the cat will rid the house of mice – but only because it catches them – not because the mice are afraid to come up from their homes beneath the floor boards! . . . The truth is, they have no sense of danger at all: they belong to the same school as those who would gladly sup with the devil regardless of a long spoon!'

Henry describes Methuselah as very much 'a *person*', disliking vulgarity, appreciative of kindnesses, and highly selective in that he chose the Fearons' young daughter, Mary, as his special friend. It was only when she appeared that he darted out of his little nest, paws on the glass, waiting to be picked out from his cage. 'His hearing, too, was excellent, for he would always know when his friend was coming: a movement from outside the room, scarcely audible to any of us, would be heard immediately; and the pink eyes would be poised ready, waiting for the moment when the door would open and his friend appear.' He might have been playing perfectly happily in one of Henry's pockets when Mary came into the room, then instantly he would emerge, jump to the floor, and run to her.

This lightning recognition seemed to indicate a good retentive memory, but experiments over a long period never bore this out. Indeed, the Fearons reluctantly reached the conclusion that Methuselah, had he been human, 'would certainly have gone to town with only one sock on. If you moved his cage, he couldn't find it without help, and even if you moved the cage to exactly the same spot ten times in succession, he still couldn't find it.

As an example of Methuselah's dislike of vulgarity, both in behaviour and in personal appearance, Henry relates: 'A jolly, red-faced man with a leering eye and a raucous voice, used to appear at Craigavad occasionally to perform odd jobs about the house and garden. He would lean his bicycle against the garage wall underneath

Methuselah's glass cage upon the shelf; and Methuselah at first came out to look at him. Through the glass window he could see a round, red face, large eyes, and a row of uneven teeth – all peering at him. "Mousey, Mousey, Mousey!" boomed a great gruff voice, as a huge ham-like hand came up to knock against the glass. For a moment, Methuselah stood transfixed, then – almost literally with his tail between his legs – he fled into the quiet of his nest, refusing to appear again.'

Henry comments that he would not have bothered to record this event were it not for the fact that mice are easily the most inquisitive of all animals. 'In the ordinary way, Methuselah would have overcome his fright (had it been fright) in a matter of minutes, and he would have been out again to look at the strange creature who had bellowed at him; but not even the tip of Methuselah's nose reappeared and we were all convinced that he had been upset by the distinct vulgarity of his visitor!'

Methuselah's days at Craigavad were long and happy right from the hour when Henry gave him to the little girl who was to prove his greatest friend. Henry recalls how, quivering with delight, Mary asked: 'Is this really mine? Oh, is he *really* mine?'

It is refreshing to find that a great cat-lover like Henry Fearon can also care for mice. He has written a poem entitled *The Secret*, about a cat and a mouse, that reads:

   The Cat has kept his secret to this day,
 Ill-treated and unloved, he served an inn
 As scavenger; surviving as he may
 The kicks of drunken merchants rich in sin.

 One night, he gave chase to a mouse at play,
 Long-tailed, so small, so beautiful and thin,
 Who ran for safety 'mid the stable hay',
 Which pleased the Cat who knew that he must win

A Child lay in the manger for a bed
And in His Hand, as if within a frame,
The prey was sleeping, freed of all its dread.
And, wondrous God, the Cat was filled with shame.

He licked with love the tiny creature's head,
And vanished ere the host of shepherds came.

* * *

Even hard businessmen can become soft-hearted over the accommodation problems of pet mice. *The Times* of London for November 17, 1988, beneath the heading in large type 'MORTGAGE TO HELP BOY'S PET MICE' reported:

'A boy has been given a mortgage to buy a new house for his pregnant pet mice, Pinky and Perky. Mark Evans, aged seven, wrote to the Halifax Building Society asking for a £28 home loan because "my mice are expecting baby mice and they need a bigger house".

The building society agreed to the interest-free loan, to be paid off at 10p a week, after examining his financial situation. Mark, who lives in Wigston Magna, Leicestershire, and earns 30p a week pocket money, said: "I think I can afford that because I don't eat many sweets".

Mr Paul Roberts, society manager, said: "We will be sending a surveyor and a valuer along with Mark to make sure it's good value and is structurally sound".'

* * *

When, as 'Fieldfare', Henry Fearon prepared a walk for the *Evening News* readers, he had to take care not to lead his faithful followers along paths dreamed of as being public ones. In his book, *Mark My Footsteps*, he wrote that there was a very famous lady who grew tired of the villagers using an old churchway as a right of way, and so she ordered the fiercest-looking tiger she could get from some menagerie. 'The savage beast was brought down to her estate, and every day, from Monday to Saturday, it was tethered in the churchway; but on Sunday morning it was led away, and the good villagers could proceed along the path to church. It was a salutary lesson, and the pity is the wild beast lived so short a while; but by a strange misfortune (no one can imagine how it happened) it ate some morsel that was bad for it, and died of poisoning.' Henry adds that this lady on one memorable occasion attended the Duke of Beaufort's hunt riding on an elephant.

Invaluable to Henry before deciding when to set out walking would have been a reliable weather prophet. There was one whom he found infallible in winter – his old black cat Tom who normally remained by the fireside for much of that season, but sometimes he rose suddenly and started dancing in an astonishing manner, leaping and gyrating, doing entrechats and fouettes as if auditioning for the musical, *Cats*. He was performing his 'Snow Dance' and within a few hours of his doing this some heavy snow would always fall.

7

LITERARY COMPANIONS

Sir Walter Scott had a remarkable cat, Hinse, and there was trouble when in April, 1816, he added to his family at Abbotsford 'a most romantic inmate – a large bloodhound' as he wrote in a letter to cat-loving Joanna Baillie, a fellow author. Scott continues: 'He is between the deer-greyhound and mastiff, with a shaggy mane like a lion, and always sits beside me at dinner, his head as high as the back of my chair; yet it will gratify you to know that Hinse keeps him in the greatest possible order, and insists upon all rights of precedence, and scratches with impunity the nose of an animal who would make no bones of a wolf . . . I heard my friend set up some most piteous howls, and I assure you the noise was no joke, occasioned by his fear of passing puss, who had stationed himself on the stairs.'

Not only Maida, the bloodhound, but Camp, the bull terrier, the two Dandy Dinmont terriers, Hamlet the jet-black greyhound, the spaniels, and Douglas on whom Scot based Lufra – 'the fleetest hound in all the North' – in *The Lady of the Lake*, all of these and others were dominated by Hinse the tom, who had his portrait painted together with Scott and Maida a number of times. But whereas the cat loved to sit for the artist, Maida often grew tired of the posing and would howl and run off.

When Maida closed his eyes for good, he was succeeded by a staghound, Nimrod, who refused to be ruled by Hinse, now a centenarian in human terms, and one day in a temper he attacked him. The tom fought back with spirit but was killed by his much younger adversary. Conveying the news to a friend, John Richardson, Scott wrote: 'Alack-a-day, my poor cat Hinse, my acquaintance, and in some sort my friend of fifteen years, was snapped at even by the paynim Nimrod. What could I say to him but what Brantôme said to some ferrailleur who had been too successful in a duel. *"Ah! mon grand ami, vous avez tué mon autre grand ami!"*'

Sir Walter Scott's favourite dog was Camp to whom there are several references in the reminiscences of his son-in-law, J G Lockhart. Camp was 'very handsome, very intelligent, and naturally very fierce, but gentle as a lamb among the children'. Scott would talk to him as if he understood what was being said, and he certainly acted as if he did. By 1809 Camp had become incapable of accompanying his master on rides. Lockhart wrote: 'At Ashestiel, as the servant was laying the cloth for dinner, he would address the dog lying on his mat before the fire and say, "Camp, my good fellow, the Sheriff's coming home by the ford – or by the hill"; and the sick animal would immediately bestir himself to welcome his master, going out by the back door or the front door, according to the direction given, and advancing as far as he was able . . .'

Camp died that year and was buried in the little garden, immediately opposite to the window at which Scott usually sat writing. 'My wife tells me she remembers the whole family standing in tears as her father himself smoothed down the turf above Camp with the saddest expression of face she had ever seen in him. He had been engaged to dine abroad that day, but apologised on account of "the death of a dear friend".'

Scott himself was later to write: 'I have sometimes

thought of the final cause of dogs having such short lives and I am quite satisfied it is in compassion to the human race; for if we suffer so much in losing a dog after an acquaintance of ten or twelve years, what would it be if they were to live double that time?'

* * *

Some regard it as an immutable law of nature that cats and dogs should not get on together. Others have proved the opposite. A hundred years previously, in 1709, Richard Steele in one of his Bickerstaff letters wrote about his little dog and cat: 'They both of them sit by my fire every night, expecting my coming home with impatience; and at my entrance, never fail of running up to me, and bidding me welcome, each of them in his proper language. As they have been bred up together from their infancy, and seen no other company, they have learned each other's manners, so that the dog often gives himself the airs of a cat, and the cat, in several of her motions and gestures, affects the behaviour of the little dog . . .'

There have been some extraordinary friendships between animals of different kinds and far odder than that between cats and dogs. W H Hudson in *A Shepherd's Life* mentions Rough, a large shaggy bitch who was a clever, good all-rounder at minding sheep. At one time when she had a litter of pups at home she was yet compelled to spend a great part of the day with the flock of ewes as they could not manage without her. The boys just then were bringing up a motherless lamb and to feed it during the day were obliged to catch a ewe with milk. The lamb trotted at Caleb, the child shepherd's heels, and once when it was crying to be fed and Rough happened to be sitting close by, it occurrred to him that her milk might serve as well as a sheep's. So the lamb was put to her and took very happily to its canine foster mother. Rough submitted patiently to the trial and the lamb adopted the sheepdog as its mother and sucked her milk several times every day.

Unfortunately, attempts to make pets live in peace with one another do not always succeed. The Empress Wu who reigned in China from AD 683 was extremely worried by the civil wars that kept breaking out, so she decided to set the people an example. With the help of her official censor, P'eng-Hsien-Chieh, she trained her cat to eat off the same plate as her parrot. A grand exhibition was held to display this example of peaceful co-existence to the unruly chieftains. It failed, because the cat misbehaved and bit off the head of the parrot.

'Mamma loves morals – Papa loves cats'

Learning that Mark Twain was a cat lover, the Editor of the *St Nicholas Magazine* wrote seeking information about the novelist's cats and Twain replied: 'I don't know as there is anything of continental or international interest to communicate about these cats. They had no history. They did not distinguish themselves in any way. They died early – on account of being so overweighed with their names, it was thought – "Sour Mash", "Apollinaris", "Zoroaster", "Blatherskite" – names given them, not in an unfriendly spirit, but merely to practise the children in large and difficult styles of pronunciation. It was a very happy idea – I mean, for the children.'

Twain travelled far and wide, and his keen eye rarely missed anything out of the ordinary such as when he visited the Zoo of Marseilles and found that the boon companion of the colossal elephant there was a common cat. He wrote: 'This cat had a fashion of climbing up the elephant's hind legs, and roosting on his back. She would sit there, with her paws curved under her breast, and sleep in the sun half the afternoon. It used to annoy the elephant at first, and he would reach up and take her down, but she would go aft and climb up again. She persisted until she finally conquered the elephant's prejudices, and now they are inseparable friends. The cat plays about her comrade's forefeet or his trunk often, until dogs approach, and then she goes aloft out of danger. The elephant has annihilated several dogs lately that pressed his companion too closely.'

Mark Twain maintained that no home could be regarded as perfect unless it had 'a well-fed, well-petted, and properly revered cat'. He also asserted that if man could be crossed with the cat, it would improve man but deteriorate the cat. His daughter Susy once said: 'The difference between Papa and Mamma is that Mamma loves morals and Papa loves cats.'

Another author's wife who disliked intensely his cats was Jane Carlyle. In fact, the term 'cat and dog' life could aptly be used to describe their home life. On the other hand, Thomas Carlyle's cat, Columbine, and Jane's dog, Nero, were the best of friends. In 1865, Jane wrote to the housemaid:

'I still hope he may not come till I myself am home first. But — if he should — there is one thing you must attend to, and which you would not think of without being told — that cat! I wish she were dead! But I can't shorten her days because, you see, my poor dear wee dog liked her! Well! There she is — and as long as she attends Mr C at his meals (she doesn't care a snuff of tobacco for him at any other times!) so long will Mr C continue to give her bits of meat, and dribbles of milk, to the ruination of carpets and hearth-rugs! I have over and over again pointed out to him the stains she has made — but he won't believe them her doing! And the dining-room carpet was so old and ugly that it wasn't worth rows with one's husband about! Now, however, that nice new cloth must be protected against the Cat-abuse. So what I wish is that you would shut up the creature when Mr C has breakfast, or dinner, or tea. And if he remarks on her absence, say it was my express desire. He has no idea what a selfish, immoral, improper beast she is, nor what mischief she does to the carpets.'

* * *

In the 18th century, Boswell wrote: 'I never shall forget the indulgence with which Dr. Johnson treated Hodge, his cat; for whom he himself used to go out and buy oysters, lest the servants, having that trouble, should take a dislike to the poor creature.' Like Mrs Carlyle, Boswell had an antipathy to cats which he admits. 'So I am uneasy when I am in the room with one, and I own I frequently suffered a good deal from the presence of the said Hodge. I recalled him one day scrambling up Dr Johnson's breast apparently with much satisfaction, while my friend, smiling and half-whistling, rubbed down his back and pulled him by the tail, and when I observed he was a fine cat, saying: "Why yes, sir, but I have had cats better than this," and then, perceiving Hodge to be out of countenance, adding: "But he is a fine cat – a very fine cat." '

Boswell adds that when he told his friend that he had heard of 'a young gentleman of good family' who was running about town shooting cats, Johnson was very concerned and cried: 'But Hodge shan't be shot – no, no, Hodge shall not be shot!'

A cat called Calvin

The American journalist, Charles Dudley Warner, in a best selling collection of sketches, *My Summer in a Garden*, wrote at length about his favourite cat which he named Calvin on account of 'his gravity, morality and uprightness'. After the pet's demise in 1880, his master recorded a detailed study of the large Angora's character.

'Calvin was as graceful in every movement as a young leopard. When he stood up to open a door − he opened all doors with old-fashioned latches − he was portentously tall, and when he stretched on the rug before the fire he seemed too long for this world − as indeed he was. His coat was the finest and softest I have ever seen, a shade of quiet Maltese, and from his throat downward, underneath, to the white of his feet, he wore the whitest and most delicate ermine . . . his face was handsome, and the expression exceedingly intelligent . . . I never saw him exactly angry, though I have seen his tail grow to an enormous size when a strange cat appeared upon his lawn . . .

'Occasionally there would be heard a night concert in the shrubbery. Calvin would ask to have the door opened, and then you would hear a rush and a "pestzt", and the concert would explode, and Calvin would quietly come in and resume his seat on the hearth − he wouldn't have any of that about the house.'

Regarding his diet, Calvin was determined to get the best. 'He would refuse beef if turkey was to be had; and if there were oysters, he would wait over the turkey to see if the oysters would not be forthcoming. And yet he was not a gross gourmand; he would eat bread if he saw me eating it, and thought he was not being imposed on. His habits of eating, also were refined; he never used a knife, and he would put up his hand and draw the fork down to his mouth as gracefully as a grown person. He would not eat in the kitchen, but insisted on his meals in the dining-room . . . They used to say that he preferred as his table-cloth on the floor a certain well-known church journal — but this was said by an Episcopalian . . . He could help himself in many ways. There was a furnace register in a retiring room where he used to go when he wished to be alone, that he always opened when he desired more heat, but never shut it, any more than he shut the door after himself . . . I can see him now, standing on the sill, looking about at the sky as if he were thinking whether it was worth while to take an umbrella, until he was near having his tail shut in . . . He had his limitations. Whatever passion he had for nature, he had no conception of art. There was sent to him once a fine and very expressive cat's head in bronze, by Fremiet. I placed it upon the floor. He regarded it intently, approached it cautiously, touched it with his nose, perceived the fraud, turned away abruptly, and never would notice it afterwards.'

Gautier – Baudelaire

Théophile Gautier, one of the leading poets of the French Romantic Movement, wrote in *La Ménagerie Intime* about his life with the many cats he kept. Madame Théophile was a dainty, red one with white breast, pink nose, and blue eyes, who slept at the foot of his bed, snoozed on the arm of his chair while he was writing, accompanied him on his walks, sat next to him at meal-times and often appropriated tasty titbits on their way from his plate to his mouth.

One day, a friend of Gautier's, who was going out of Paris for a few days, left a pet parrot in his care. Madame Théophile had never seen such a bird before and was mystified. The poet wrote: 'She gazed at it with an air of profound meditation seeking enlightenment from the knowledge of natural history she had picked up on the roofs, the yard, and the garden. Her thoughts were reflected in her eyes and I was able to read in them the result of her examination: "It is unmistakably a chicken." Having reached this conclusion, she sprang from the table on which she had posted herself to make her investigations, and crouched down in one corner of the room, flat on her stomach, her elbows out, her head low, her muscular backbone on the stretch . . . The parrot followed her movements with feverish anxiety, fluffing out its feathers, rattling its chain, lifting its foot and moving its claws, and sharpening its beak upon the edge of its seed-box. Its instinct warned that an enemy was preparing to attack.'

The eyes of the cat plainly said: 'Green though it is, that chicken must be good to eat.' Gautier says that he watched fascinated, ready to interfere when necessary. 'Madame Théophile gloated with anticipation like a gourmet sitting down to enjoy a truffled pullet. Suddenly she arched her back like a bow being drawn and landed right upon the perch. The parrot in desperation called out unexpectedly in a sonorous bass voice: "Have you had your breakfast, Jack?"

'The words filled the cat with indescribable terror, and she leapt down. The blast of a trumpet, the smashing of a pile of crockery, or a pistol-shot fired in her ear would not have disturbed her to such an extent. "And what did you have?" went on the parrot. The cat's expression now clearly meant: "This isn't a bird – it's a man – it speaks."'

The parrot bawled out from its repertoire in a deafening voice, for it had at once realised that the terror caused by its speech was its surest means of defence. Madame Théophile looked at her master questioningly and his reply proving unsatisfactory, she sneaked under the bed and refused to come out for the rest of the day.

Gautier adds that this cat also had a taste for music. 'Nestling upon a pile of scores, she would listen attentively and with every mark of satisfaction to the singers who came to perform at my piano. But high notes made her nervous, and she never failed to close the singer's mouth with her paw if the lady sang the high A. We used to try the experiment for fun, and it never failed once. It was quite impossible to fool my dilettante cat on that note.'

Gautier's cats doted on perfumes. Madame Théophile would go into 'ecstasies on breathing in the patchouli and vetiver used for Cashmere shawls' and in all cats he found that the odour of valerian brought on a kind of 'epileptic ecstasy'. Another of his pets, immaculately white and majestic, was called Don Pierrot de Navarre, and seated close to the fire looked as if he understood the conversation of Gautier and his friends and 'every now and then would utter a little cry as if to object and give his own opinion upon literature, which formed our chief topic'.

Don Pierrot was very fond of books. 'When he found one open on the table, he would lie down by it, gaze attentively at the page and turn the leaves with his claws; then he ended by going to sleep, just as if he had been reading a fashionable novel. As soon as I picked up my pen, he would leap upon the desk and watch the steel nib scribbling away on the paper, moving his head every time I began a new line. Sometimes he endeavoured to collaborate with me, and would snatch the pen out of my hand, no doubt with the intention of writing in his turn. . . .'

Gautier writes that Don Pierrot always awaited his return at night, and as soon as he came in would rub against his legs, purr, escort him to his bedroom, wait until he had undressed, jump up on the bed, put paws

round his neck, massage his nose, lick him 'with his tiny
red tongue, rough as a file, and utter little inarticulate
cries by way of expressing the pleasure he felt at seeing
me again'. Then the cat used to perch upon the
backboard of the bed and sleep there like a bird roosting
on a branch.

Don Pierrot's companion, Séraphite, was also snow-
white. 'Of a dreamy and contemplative disposition, she
would remain for hours on a cushion, following with
intense attention sights invisible to ordinary mortals.
She liked to be petted, but would show no appreciation
of it except in the case of the few people of whom she
approved — and even then only perfunctorily. She loved
luxury, and we were always sure to find her curled up
in the newest armchair or on the piece of stuff that best
set off her swansdown coat. She spent endless time at
her toilet . . . If anyone touched her, she at once
smoothed the spot, for she could not bear to be rumpled
. . . Among her own kind she must have been a duchess
at the very least.'

These two white cats bore three coal-black kittens
called Enjolras, Gavroche and Eponine, after characters
in Victor Hugo's *Les Misérables*. The eldest and handsomest had a lion-like head, well-whiskered cheeks, and
a tail like a fluffy feather duster. Gavroche was smaller
'with a sharp, satirical look' and had the habit of seizing
every opportunity to join in the streets 'numbers of
wandering cats of lineage low, with whom he took part
in performances of doubtful taste . . . Sometimes he
would bring in to his meals, in order to treat them, consumptive friends of his, so starved that every rib in their
body showed, whom he had picked up, for he was a kind-
hearted fellow.' Eponine was more lissom and slender
than her brother, with a long face, slanting green eyes
and incessantly moving whiskers. 'There never was a
more sensitive, nervous and electric animal. If she were
stroked two or three times in the dark, blue sparks came

87

crackling from her fur. She attached herself to me in particular . . . She trots up when she hears the bell ring, welcomes my visitors, leads them into the drawing-room, shows them to a seat, talks to them with croonings and cooings and whimpers quite unlike the language cats make use of among themselves, and which simulates the articulate speech of man. She says, in the plainest possible fashion: "Don't be impatient – look at the pictures, or chat with me, if you enjoy that. My master will be down in a minute." And when I come in, she discreetly retires to an armchair or the top of the piano, and listens to the conversation without breaking in upon it, like a well-bred animal that is used to society.'

Théophile Gautier's daughter, Judith, brilliant poet, novelist and playwright, also worshipped cats and hers included Satan, a Persian with incandescent eyes. In her autobiography, she wrote that when a girl all her father's cats joined them at table for meals. A bell would be rung and ahead of anyone else Eponine would leap on to her chair next to Judith's sister, whilst Enjolras stationed herself beside Judith. And both would survey with greedy gleaming eyes the food on their plates waiting for Théophile to be seated and signal to them that they might start eating.

No French writer was fonder of cats and understood their characters better than Baudelaire, whom Théophile Gautier has described as 'a voluptuous wheedling cat himself, with velvety manners'. He was ridiculed in the popular press. One account reads: 'On visiting anyone for the first time, both socially and on business, he won't settle down until he has seen the household cat. Then when it is brought to him, he picks it up tenderly, kisses it many times, and gives it his whole attention, failing to answer anything said to him.'

* * *

Champfleury, author of arguably the finest book on cats, *Les Chats*, has written how he and Baudelaire would often walk the streets of Paris seeking cats to admire. They stopped at the doors of laundries to gaze at those luxuriously curled up on piles of beautifully finished white linen and that were revelling in the fragrance of the newly-ironed fabrics. 'Into what fits of contemplation have we fallen before the windows, while the pretty, coquettish laundresses struck attitudes at the ironing-board under the impression that we were admiring them.' Should a cat appear in a doorway or cross the street, Baudelaire would coax it to come to him, fuss over it, 'sometimes stroking it the wrong way'.

In a prose piece, entitled, *L'Horloge*, Baudelaire begins by relating how the missionary, Father Evariste Huc, met a boy near a farm in China and asked him the time. 'Wait a moment,' he replied, then running away he returned with a cat in his arms, looked into its eyes and declared: 'It isn't quite midday.' Huc in his reminiscences, *The Chinese Empire*, states that on reaching the farm he and his companion asked the Chinese Christians they were visiting there whether they, too, could tell the time in this way. 'They seemed surprised, so we explained what had happened, and they immediately gave chase to all the cats in the neighbourhood. Bringing back three or four, they demonstrated how to use the creatures' eyes as watches, pointing out that the pupils grew narrower and narrower until twelve o'clock, when each one became like a fine line, as thin as a hair, drawn perpendicularly across the eyes, and that after twelve the dilation recommenced. When we had closely inspected those of all the cats at our disposal, we concluded that it was indeed past noon, as all the eyes perfectly agreed upon the point.'

Father Huc adds: 'We have had some hesitation in mentioning this Chinese discovery, as it may, doubtless, diminish the sales of watches and cause unemployment. All major discoveries tend to injure some people's interests and we hope, nevertheless, that watches will go on being made, because there will be some who cannot spare the time to run after the cat, or who may fear damage to their own eyes from too close an examination of pussy's.'

Wells – Poe – Kipling – Dickens

H G Wells had a succession of well-fed cats and was particularly attached to one that he always kept by him when there were visitors, because if anybody talked too much, it would miaow loudly and disapprovingly, then jump down from its chair, walk to the door and scratch impatiently. H G's last cat was called 'Mr Peter Wells' and once its owner corrected a stranger who had addressed this important creature as 'Master' Peter Wells.

Far from well-fed was penurious Edgar Allan Poe's tortoiseshell Catarina, which when Mrs Poe was dying in an unheated bedroom laid against her to keep her warm.

That other great short story writer, Rudyard Kipling, in *The Cat That Walked By Itself*, compared in turn man's connexions with the dog, the horse, and the cat. He suggested that, originally, the first two surrendered their liberty in exchange for food and security, but the cat contracted to catch mice and rats for humans and be their children's best friends, and in exchange cats would be fed milk and made welcome by all firesides. Apart from this, the feline race would be free to do whatever they pleased.

Charles Dickens owned a cat (daughter of Wilhelmina, by mistake originally named William) which from when she was a kitten never wanted to leave him for the fireside and would lie in his lap as he wrote or read. One winter's evening, he was working at his desk when the light from the candlestick on it was abruptly extinguished. As he stuck a match, Dickens noticed that the cat was giving him a look that seemed to complain of being neglected, so he stroked her reassuringly before picking up his pen. Then, a short while later, the light began to fail and reacting at once, he caught puss in the act of covering the flame with her paw. She stared entreatingly at him and, unable to resist he surrendered to her wiles and, putting aside his papers, gave her his entire attention. She purred triumphantly as he fondled her.

Pets feature in several of Dickens's novels. In *Bleak House*, we meet Krook's tigerish cat, Lady Jane, Miss Flite's garret companions of larks, linnets and goldfish, and Mr Boythorn's tiny canary about whom he says: 'By heaven, he is the most astonishing bird in Europe. I wouldn't take ten thousand guineas for that bird. I have left an annuity for his sole support, in case he should outlive me. He is, in sense and attachment, a phenomenon. And his father before him was one of the most astonishing birds that ever lived!'

In *Barnaby Rudge*, we have Dickens's 'knowing imp' of a raven listening to conversations 'with a polite attention and a most extraordinary appearance of comprehending every word'. With his head very much on one side, and his bright eye shining like a diamond, he preserves a thoughtful silence for a few seconds, and then replies 'in a voice so hoarse and distant that it seems to come through his thick feathers rather than out of his mouth: "Holloa, holloa, holloa! What's the matter here? Keep up your spirits. Never say die. Bow-wow-wow. I'm a devil, I'm a devil, I'm a devil. Hurrah!" And then, as if exulting in his infernal character, he began to whistle.' Grip, who is aged one hundred and twenty, or thereabouts, never goes to sleep or so much as winks, says Barnaby. 'Why, any time of night you may see his eyes in my dark room, shining like two sparks. And every night, and all night, too, he's broad awake, talking to himself, thinking what he shall do tomorrow, where we shall go, and what he shall steal, and hide, and bury.'

Grip flutters to the floor and goes to Barnaby 'not in a hop, or walk, or run, but in a pace like that of a very particular gentleman with exceedingly tight boots on trying to walk fast over loose pebbles'. Then, stepping into Barnaby's extended hand, and condescending to be held out at arm's length, Grip 'gave vent to a succession of sounds not unlike the drawing of some eight or ten dozen of long corks' and his owner, taking him in his arms, rolls about with him on the floor.

In *Nicholas Nickleby*, Dickens claims: 'There was not a bird of such methodical and business-like habits in all the world as the blind blackbird who dreamed and dozed away his days in a large, snug cage, and had lost his voice, from old age, years before Tim first bought him.' Timothy Linkinwater had actually acquired Dick out of compassion. Distressed by the creature's starved and suffering condition, his intention had been originally to humanely end such a wretched life, but he had decided to wait three days and, before half that time was out, the bird did revive and continued to do so. And thus Dick came to keep old Tim company as he worked as a clerk in the Brothers Cheeryble's counting-house, where he introduces the new young book-keeper, Nicholas Nickleby, to the pet which 'thrusting his bill between the bars, turns his sightless head towards his old master; and at that moment it would be very difficult to determine which of the two was the happier – the bird or Tim Linkinwater'.

Dickens's dogs in his novels include Diogenes given by Mr Toots to Florence Dombey, Dora Spenlow's Jip in *David Copperfield*, a lap dog with the habit of walking about the table-cloth during dinner and putting his foot in the salt or melted butter and who, muffled in a towel, is put in a plate warmer to deaden his howling and barking, while in the *Pickwick Papers*, the stranger tells

Mr Winkle that he should keep dogs, adding: 'Dog of my own once – pointer – surprising instinct – out shooting one day – entering enclosure – whistled – dog stopped – whistled again – Ponto – no go; stock still – called him, Ponto, Ponto – wouldn't move – dog transfixed – staring at a board – looked up, saw an inscription: "Game keeper has orders to shoot all dogs found in this enclosure" – wouldn't pass it – wonderful dog – valuable dog that – very . . . Hundred more anecdotes of the same animal.'

But the most memorable dog in Dickens's novels is, of course, the mongrel Bull's Eye, who dies tragically with his master, Bill Sikes.

'Saki' and his tigers

H H Munro, the author who wrote as 'Saki', assembled around him a variety of strange pets. When living in Burma, corresponding with his sister, he revealed that his boon companion was a tiger kitten – an exhibitionist that enjoyed romping around whenever its owner was watching. An old lady arrived and occupied the bedroom next to Munro's in the hotel where he was staying. 'I was rather astonished when the proprietor came that evening, and with great nervousness, said that she was – er – er – a fidgety old lady and – er – er – er – there was a door connecting our rooms. I was quite mystified as to what he was driving at, but I answered languidly that the door was locked on my side and there was a box against it, so she could not possibly break in. The proprietor collapsed and retired in confusion. I afterwards remembered that the "cub" has spent a large portion of the afternoon pretending that this door was a besieged city, and it was a battering ram. And it does throw such vigour into its play.'

Munro met the old lady at dinner and was greeted with an icy stare 'which was refreshing in such a climate'. That night the tiger kitten began to roar the moment Munro went to bed. The more he tried to comfort it the more inconsolable it grew. 'The situation was awful – in my room a noise like the lion-house at 4 p.m., while on the other side of the wall rose the beautiful litany of the Church of England. Then I heard the rapid turning of leaves. She was evidently searching for Daniel to gain strength from the perusal of the lion's den story; only she couldn't find Daniel so fell back upon Psalms of David. As for me, I fled, and sent my boy to take the cage down to the stable. When I returned, I heard words in the next room that never came out of the Psalms; words such as no lady ought to use; but then it is annoying to be woken out of your first sleep by a rendering of "Jamrach's Evening Hymn". She left . . .'

Some months later, commenting on the news that his sister had acquired a Persian kitten, Munro wrote back: 'Of course, I, who have the untameable carnivora of the jungle roaming in savage freedom through my rooms, cannot feel any interest in mere domestic cats, but I am not intolerant and I have no objection to your keeping one or two. My beast sleeps on a shelf in its cage all day, but comes out after dinner and plays the giddy goat all over the place. I should like to get another wild cat to chum with it, there are several species in Burma: the jungle-cat, the bay-cat, the lesser leopard-cat, the tiger-cat, marbled-cat, spotted wild-cat, and rusty-spotted cat; the latter, I have read, make delightful pets.'

Beverley Nichols' cats

Beverley Nichols was a great cat lover and wrote entertainingly about his own. Having been Dame Nellie

Melba's secretary it was only natural that feline behaviour should remind him of that of prima donnas. The savage expression on his pet Oscar's face as he watched sparrows in the garden through the window brought back memories of a performance of *Norma* at La Scala with Callas in the title rôle that Nichols had attended. Seated in a box with a prima donna on either side of him, he joined in the ovation that the audience gave Callas as she ended the aria, *Casta diva* – but the expression on the two ladies' faces was exactly like Oscar's. They were contorted with rage and envy, and if Callas had been a bird 'her days would have been short indeed'. Similarly, faced with another cat, Four, doing a *danse macabre* on the lawn with a mouse – 'pouncing and retreating and cavorting' – made him think of Salomé's antics with the head of John the Baptist.

Nichols says that he always tried to rescue the mouse. On one occasion when Oscar was the offender, his master pursued him along a hedge, banging a frying-pan with a brick and shouting: 'Put it down – put that wretched thing down!' Unfortunately, on the other side of the hedge was a lane along which ladies from the local Conservative Association were parading on their way to the village hall. They were carrying a blue banner bearing the motto, 'For Queen and Country'. They misunderstood Beverley Nichols's behaviour and he says he was never asked to open their garden fête again.

The felines called One, Two, and Three had all been Siamese and had died of flu when kittens. Four was a black tom with 'an exquisite purr, a perfect vibrato, super breath control, and exceptional range'. Four disliked jazz and if any records of it were played, he would rise from the chair where he had been lying and, casting a look of disgust at the instrument from which the sounds were emanating, he would stalk out of the room. He loved to listen to Nichols at the piano playing

Chopin and Greig. When his master moved to Ham Cottage, Four made the top of the tool-shed his watch tower where in the autumn if it were not for him warning off the squirrels by lashing his tail, Nichols would never have had any nuts from the old walnut tree.

Four, from kittenhood, concluded that the best tactics to employ to obtain for himself more than anybody else was to pretend he was being treated like an orphan in a Dickensian workhouse. Shouldn't he get what he wanted, he would at once assume a look of terror, and make off with such an air that an eye witness, says Nichols, would assume master was a hard-hearted cat beater. Coughing was a highly impressive part of Four's act. Should his dish of fish not please him, he would sniff, jerk backwards and then, providing he had an audience, give a cough worthy of the finest actress performing the consumptive dying Mimi. Any stranger, Four hoped, would take him for a wretched, neglected creature almost at his last gasp, whose untimely end could only be averted 'by a swiftly opened tin of tongue'. It was all most professionally timed and 'the only reason it was not quite heart-rending is that Four, like many other Mimis whom one has seen expiring in Act 4 of *La Bohème*, is exceedingly plump'.

The cat known as Five, although the plumpest, had the smallest appetite, eating slowly and haughtily, and spent such long periods of time sitting before a mirrored wall staring into his own green eyes that when he eventually tore himself away he looked quite dopey. When Six, a beautiful ginger, was called by that name it sounded too much like 'Sick' so he was rechristened 'Seven'. Oscar ought to have been 'Eight' but he had already been given his name before Nichols acquired him, and proving with his white chest to be a cat of strong individuality, any change of name would have been 'unthinkable'.

Val Geilgud and Bernard Levin

Val Gielgud, playwright and BBC luminary, had an exceptional assortment of cats. Lulu, a Siamese given him by Compton Mackenzie, called after the character in *Extraordinary Women*, did all she could to surpass the sexual record of D H Lawrence's original. Gielgud claimed to have done his utmost to mate her respectably with various aristocrats of her own breed, but she ignored and even attacked them, preferring to copulate with riffraff — 'rusty black toms, battered tabby toms, half-starved ginger toms, parti-coloured gladiators of unimaginable ancestry' — and conceiving dozens of kittens totally unlike their mother apart from her voice.

Dorothy Sayers delivered, at Gielgud's Long Acre flat in a hat-box, Merlin, son of a 'pensive witch', warning the new owner that in view of such an ancestry he would have to be treated with due deference. Gielgud soon found that the creature's large unwinking yellow eyes could detect more in the place than he could. Merlin would sit very still ever so long, his attention rivetted on some particular spot. 'Then his hackles would rise. He would growl deep in his throat.' And sometimes he would leap up, half apprehensively, at something invisible to humans in the air.

Merlin made it clear that he found life in a flat restrictive by spending more and more time scrambling up book-cases, so one weekend Gielgud took him on a visit to friends in the country, where he at once made for the trees outside, and settling on the topmost branches refused to come down. Eventually a ladder had to be obtained so that he could be captured and taken back to Long Acre, where his book-case scaling became so frequent and damaging that Gielgud was driven in despair into boarding him out in deepest Kent. Here an orchard provided him with tremendous scope for gymnastics.

The Siamese Gielgud loved second best, named Hugo, was country born and bred and enjoyed robust health. He carried on like a passionate and possessive mistress, sleeping beside Val and rousing him in the morning by nibbling his ear. In the evenings, immediately Hugo heard the sound of master's opening the front door, he would gambol along the passage to meet him. He expected a reasonable ration of chit-chat and caresses after so many hours of separation and, if this was not forthcoming to his satisfaction, he would flounce round the room by way of the mantelpiece and the tops of furniture, kicking ornaments and photographs on to the floor with a hind leg.

When the Second World War broke out and Gielgud's department at Broadcasting House was moved to Evesham, Hugo accompanied him there, and as the people on whom Gielgud was billeted did not get on with Hugo, a furnished house was rented for the pet's comfort. Then at the end of 1939, Val Gielgud was transferred to Manchester and had to live at the Midland Hotel, so Hugo was taken care of by a friend in London, where he died during the 1944 epidemic of 'cat flu'. He was later succeeded by Merlin II.

Other feline pets of Val Gielgud's included Black Out, a tabby, who arrived mysteriously over the roofs during one air-raid and disappeared as mysteriously a fortnight later during another raid – Blitz, lean and black, with a spitfire purr like the sound of an anti-aircraft battery – Daffodil, the only Siamese he knew that liked eating bananas – and, best loved of all, U-puss from Peking, cigar-coloured, with eyes of beryl green and large, bat-like ears, that would ride on Gielgud's shoulder when he went to watch the polo at Cowdray Park, and who was more amused than apprehensive when the miscellany of dogs present barked and yapped at his strange appearance.

Bernard Levin has written most engagingly about his

cats. In *The Lives and Times of Smoky Dostoievski and Others*, published in *The Times* on February 13, 1973, he declared that he had enjoyed the company of so many remarkable cats in his life that it was difficult to select one as the most outstanding. However, although over thirty years had passed, he still regarded his very first, a superb Persian called Tim, as the noblest and handsomest of all with hearing so keen that he always heard the sound of the approaching cat's-meat man long before anyone else. Tim would take his naps in the shop window, lying so elegantly still that frequently people strolling by would come in to ask whether the feline beauty was alive or some miracle of a taxidermist's art. Levin's grandfather would then cry 'Tim!' and Tim (who was fully aware of what was going on) would jump from the window and rub himself against the admirer's legs.

Tim lived to a great age, surviving innumerable disasters such as 'being frozen solid' one winter's night when he refused to come in, and even an attempt to murder him with poison by a wicked neighbour. He was luckier than the shop cat before him, who expired after falling into a pot of paint, and than his successor who was run over by a car. Bernard Levin says that the next few cats in his life weren't in the same class as Tim, one was even terrified of mice. Then one day they found on the doorstep a kitten barely four inches in length which some brute had kicked in the face, rendering it lopsided. As no cat in distress has ever been refused aid by Levin or any member of his family, the creature was allowed in and fed. Then to avoid the risk of being ejected, he crept under the stove and obstinately remained there for three days. So he was adopted and called simply, 'Cat'.

Cat, when he grew up, did not recover from his disfigurement. Fortunately, this did not appear to trouble him though he looked odd, as a length of pink tongue drooped unretractably from the corner of his mouth. One day, snoozing in the sun above the front porch, he tumbled off on to the ground, hitting his head and biting off the dangling piece of tongue. To everyone's amazement, all Cat did was to let out another length of tongue which projected to the same extent as previously, though its tip was now curved inwards in shape.

It seems that Cat was prone to such accidents, for later he slipped off a window ledge two floors up, but though he appeared to escape injury Bernard Levin thought he was never quite right in his upper storey after that. Later, as a consequence of this mishap, he suffered so much with pains in his jaw that they considered ending his days, but the vet reassured them, insisting that he would be a new cat once all his teeth were extracted, which proved the case. The only ill effect was cosmetic. The fact that the two canine teeth were left together with his by then very misshapen features made him resemble 'a feline Dracula'. Happily, Cat had no difficulty eating 'though he never learnt the trick of doing so with his paw like the one in the television advertisement'.

8

PETS IN CHURCH

The Medici Pope Leo X, great patron of the arts, assembled in Rome the finest zoo of his times. King Manoel of Portugal was also a collector of remarkable animals and on a visit to the pontiff, he took with him as gifts a huge elephant, two exceptional leopards, and a tame panther mounted on a Persian horse's back. A rhinoceros would have been included as well had not the ship conveying it capsized under the weight. Spectators have described the pageantry staged by Manoel, as he and his bizarre presents went through Rome to the Castle of St Angelo, as the most extraordinary they had ever witnessed. On reaching its entrance outside which the Pope and his Cardinals were awaiting them, the elephant respectfully dipped his trunk into an ornate pail full of perfumed water and sprayed the Holy Father and his prelates, and also the cheering crowd, as the cannon roared and the church bells rang out.

Fat cat

René de Châteaubriand, egoistic French writer and

statesman, regarded as the French Byron, doted on cats and writing to his close friend, the Comte de Marcellus, he told him that when he looked in a mirror he was struck by his own growing resemblance to one. During his time in Rome as French Ambassador, he was approached by the Pope, Leo XII, a sad, saintly man, who lived in a barely furnished room with his cat, Micetto, and ate hardly anything except a little polenta. Micetto, brought up by the Pope in a skirt of his robe, had been born at the Vatican in the Raphael Gallery. Leo said that he had noticed how much Châteaubriand admired this greyish-red cat with black stripes across it and so was going to bequeath it to him in his will. In due course, Châteaubriand inherited Micetto and cared devotedly for it in Paris. His wife, the Vicomtesse, in a letter to a M le Moine, complained that though the Pope had loved the cat, he had made it fast 'because all they knew in the Vatican in the way of sought after dishes was cod and beans'. She soon turned Micetto into a very fat cat.

* * *

Earlier on, Gregory the Great and Gregory III, pontiffs in the sixth and eighth centuries respectively, gave up all their money and other possessions, each keeping only one small cat. The sixth arrondisement in Paris had the reputation of having the largest number of cats in France, thanks to the virility of the tom cat Pope Pius VII brought with him when he attended Napoleon Bonaparte's coronation as Emperor. The present Pope, John Paul II, has kept up the tradition of these pontiffs by having breakfast in company with his pet cat.

Cardinal passion

Cardinal Richelieu, who ruled France for eighteen years in the seventeenth century, had a passion for cats, particularly kittens. Every morning when he woke, Abel and Teyssandier, the two men chosen to care for his feline friends, brought a selection of kittens for him to play with on his bed. Courtiers knew that they would be rewarded with advancement if they proved themselves to be true cat-lovers and there was intense competition among them to see who could find the most playful kitten or endearingly attractive cat to give him. When an elderly member of his household, Mlle de Gournay, retired and applied for a pension, the Cardinal granted her 200 livres. His secretary then said that something ought to be done for Mamie Paillon. 'Who's she?' demanded Richelieu. 'Her cat, and a rather delicate creature,' explained the Abbé de Boisrobert. The great minister laughed and granted an extra 20 livres. 'That's kind of your Eminence, but Mamie has some kittens,' Boisrobert pointed out, knowing that on hearing this Richelieu was sure to allow each one a *pistole*, which he did.

The Marquis de Racan was a second-rate and absent-minded poet who had a favourite cat that one day gave birth to two kittens in his best wig. On rising, Racan first donned his toupée, then on leaving to visit the Cardinal he added the wig. Hardly had he arrived than he became aware that something was moving about under the mountain of false hair, and he started scratching at it.

'What's the matter?' Richelieu asked. 'Is something irritating your scalp?'

'I don't know what it is,' the other replied, 'but for the last quarter of an hour I've been hearing a sort of buzzing in my head.'

The Cardinal was about to suggest that medical advice be sought when he started. 'Why, your wig's all askew – and it's starting to move!' And two mewing kittens fell

103

at the feet of Richelieu who, not known for a sense of humour, laughed uproariously. He added the kittens to his menagerie, naming them Racan and Perruque, and they were among the fourteen cats alive at his death and to all of whom he left pensions.

In England, Cardinal Wolsey had his cat in his arms when he gave audiences. It was with him during meals and even in church. The envoy extraordinary from the Republic of Venice wrote disapprovingly in his despatches: 'Certainly nothing like it has been seen since Caligula.'

* * *

Cardinal Capecelatro, a distinguished and popular Archbishop of Taranto in the eighteenth century, was a collector of remarkable cats. Lady Morgan, the Irish authoress and traveller, also had a number of them, headed by the magnificent and highly intelligent Ginger, who, when she prayed, would purr after every 'amen'. In her *Book of the Boudoir*, Lady Morgan describes a visit to the Italian prelate's palace in Naples. 'You must pardon my passion for cats, but I never exclude them from my dining-room, and you will find they make excellent company,' he said as he led her in.

She writes: 'Between the first and second course, the door opened, and several large and beautiful cats were introduced, by the names of Pantalone, Desdemona, Otello, and other dramatic *cognomina*. They took their places on chairs near the table, and were as silent, as quiet, as motionless, and as well behaved, as the most *bon ton* table in London would require. On the Archbishop requesting one of the chaplains to help the Signora Desdemona to something, the butler stepped up to his Lordship and observed, "Desdemona will prefer waiting for the roast."

'After dinner they were sent to walk on the terrace, and I had the honour of assisting at their *coucher*, for which a number of comfortable cushions were prepared in the Archbishop's dressing room.' She adds that her host, 'so well known through Italy as the author of many clever works, has also produced one on cats, full of ingenuity and pleasantry'.

Clerical cats

It seems astonishingly narrow-minded that a cat should be persecuted on account of the religion of its former owner, but this happened in the case of the one that George Borrow, the author and traveller, befriended when he and his family were in Llangollen. They were sitting at tea in the parlour of their lodgings and all doors were open on account of the fine weather. Then a black cat entered hastily, sat down on the carpet by the table, looked up towards them, and mewed piteously. He had never seen so wretched looking a creature. In his book, *Wild Wales*, Borrow wrote that he subsequently learnt the cat's history prior to their arrival. It had belonged to a previous Vicar of Llangollen and had been left behind at his departure. His successor brought with him dogs and cats, who, conceiving that the late Vicar's cat had no business at the Vicarage, drove it out.

Almost all the local people were dissenters, and knowing the cat to be a Church of England cat, not only would they not harbour it, but did all they could to make it miserable. 'Stone it – hang it, drown it!' they cried. The lodging-house keeper where the Borrows were staying was, he says, 'though a very excellent person, a bitter

105

dissenter, who would make after it, frequently attended by her maid and her young son, both of whom hated the cat, and were always ready to attack it, either alone or in company, and no wonder, the maid being not only a dissenter but a class teacher, and the boy not only a dissenter, but intended for the dissenting ministry . . . It had never entered the house before, even when there were lodgers . . . Did instinct draw it towards us? We gave it some bread-and-butter, and a little tea with milk and sugar. It ate and drank and soon began to purr.'

The Borrows' landlady was horrified when she saw the church cat on her carpet. 'What impudence!' she exclaimed, and made towards it, but on their telling her that they did not expect that it should be disturbed, she let it alone. 'A very remarkable circumstance was, that though the cat had hitherto been in the habit of flying not only from her face, but the very echo of her voice, it now looked her in the face with perfect composure, as much as to say, "I don't fear you, for I know that I am now safe and with my own people." It stayed with us for two hours and then went away. The next morning it returned. To be short, though it went away every night, it became our own cat, and one of our family.' George Borrow gave it something which cured its sores, and through good treatment it soon lost its other ailments and began to look sleek and well.

The question now was what to do with the cat when the Borrows left on their travels. 'At length we thought of applying to a young woman of sound church principles who was lately married . . . with whom we were slightly acquainted, to take charge of the animal, and she on the first intimation of our wish willingly acceded to it. So with her poor puss was left along with a trifle for its milk money, and with her, as we subsequently learned, it continued in peace and comfort till one morning it sprang from the hearth into the air, gave a mew and died.'

* * *

A nineteenth century Church of England clergyman who believed that animals had souls and should be admitted to divine services was Robert Stephen Hawker, Rector of Morwenstow in Cornwall, who was also a poet and a gifted writer of ballads. He would often stand at his lectern with his nine cats grouped around him. In the evening, he would lead them to the cat-house. Each waited till he uttered its name and then jumped up to the shelf on which they reposed. One he called his 'most righteous cat' because whenever he missed it he generally found it waiting at the church door. There were rumours that he had christened them all at the font in secret to make sure that they were admitted to Heaven with him.

* * *

Another Victorian clergyman, Canon Henry Parry Liddon, whose preaching drew packed congregations to St Paul's for twenty years, also doted on cats, who all had different residences assigned to them. Tweedledum and Tweedledee, handsome brothers, lived at his country home, Amen Corner, another shared his chambers in London, a fourth, Campion, was boarded out and only visited the Canon occasionally, and a fifth preferred the Common Room at Christchurch, Oxford to any other quarters. This one was reserved, rudely spurning all church dignitaries except Liddon, whom he loved to distraction and whom he delighted to entertain with acrobatic feats. According to Agnes Reppler in *The Fireside Sphinx*, the cat would jump upon a bust of a Dr Busby which stood on a bracket near the door, 'balance upon that severe and reverend brow, take a flying leap to the mantelpiece, and returning, land with exquisite and unvarying accuracy on the bust, repeating this performance as often as his master desired'. The Cannon found it great fun to stand with his back to the bracket and throw a biscuit at Dr Busby's head, 'the cat catching it dexterously, and without losing his precarious foothold'.

Pets and the hereafter

A feature of the increasingly tolerant attitude of some clergy has been the acceptance of the belief that animals have souls and that attention should therefore be paid to their religious upbringing. In the early 1960s, at a special service held at St Paul's, Covent Garden, Canon Clarence May blessed thirty animals including a black dog called Satan. Lady Violet Munnings' dog, Toby, sang a hymn that she claimed he had composed. The fact that the congregation could not make out any actual words, she attributed to his suffering from a sore throat and that an aggressive-looking Alsatian present in the front pew had upset him.

A devout resident of Halberton in the West Country arrived with her terrier, Pip, one Sunday at the parish church and not only sat throughout the service with him on her lap but shared Holy Communion with him. The Vicar reproved her. She must not do this again, but she was unrepentant, saying she would not come to church again unless her pet were allowed to take Communion. The Vicar reported the matter to his Bishop, who confirmed the ban.

Another Bishop, that of Chichester, conducted the dedication of a canine cemetry in Essex where over 2,000 dogs have been buried — some with a religious ceremony led by a clergyman.

In Rio de Janeiro at least a dozen times as many dogs have been interred with solemn candle-lit, flower bedecked rites in a scrupulously well maintained cemetery, but the Number One such shrine to pets in the whole of America must be the Haresdale Canine Cemetery in Westchester, where the approaching 50,000 graves include those of cats, monkeys, parrots, a lion, salamanders, goldfish, piglets, hens and cockerels.

The morals of Henrietta

Talking of hens, the *Telegraph Weekend Magazine* in early 1989 published an account of an interview with the orthodox Bishop of Peterborough by Alison Nadel, who talked to him and his wife in the kitchen of the Palace. They drank tea while his hen, Henrietta, sat at his feet under the table on a small brown mat, and he quietly confided that she was not really a pet, 'having no brains to speak of and a very short attention span'. She was not cuddly — if he picked her up, she panicked. But she did have 'a quality of innocence and vulnerability'. He thought it rather nice that she always welcomed him when he came in. His wife could do a great impression of her. Alison Nadel reported: ' "Pwaak, pwaack, pwaack," squawks his wife obligingly.'

Henrietta slept in a shed by the kitchen door between two big brown feather dusters. She waited by the fridge in the morning and was extremely fond of cheese and bacon. The Bishop did not believe that Henrietta shared his sense of moral responsibility. 'We had a great debate about this in one of our diocesan discussion groups,' he told Alison Nadel. 'A young curate's whippet died and he was extremely upset. And we decided that animals don't have a soul because they have no real means of responding to God. But we thought they were part of the furniture of Heaven, which is a nice image. Henrietta can't be a good hen or a bad hen. Her character is just a reflection of our feelings at a particular time.'

* * *

No one could have objected to the service held in London's Holy Trinity Church, to commemorate the passing of Faith in 1948. Her courage during the Blitz will be remembered by posterity thanks to the plaque inscribed 'The Bravest Cat in the World' set up by the PDSA in St Paul's where this stray had lived happily for the previous twelve years. It was a felicitous idea for all the children of the neighbourhood to be invited to bring their pets to the service for, as a result, the church was crowded not only with cats and dogs, kittens and puppies, but hens and ducks, a lamb, and there was even a minnow in a jam jar.

Mahomet, friend of all cats

Mahomet, the founder of Islam, was greatly attached to cats and in particular to one called Meuzza that slept on his robe, and on one occasion when summoned to his prayers, rather than disturb it he cut off the sleeve on which it was lying. He used water from which Meuzza had drunk for his purifications, and Aylshah, the favourite out of his ten wives, was allowed the privilege of eating from a vessel used by the pet. Also, when Mahomet decided to reward his follower, Abd-er-rahern, for his faithful services, he bestowed upon him the title, Abuhareira, meaning 'Father of the Cat'.

According to another story, the Prophet not only promised Meuzza that it would live for ever in Paradise but bestowed on the feline race the special dexterity of always landing on their feet, thus permanently protecting them from injury by falling over. As a result of the example this set, Mahomet's adherents opened a hospital for cats in Damascus, supported by public subscriptions.

Possibly, too, it was remembrance of Mahomet's concern for the comfort of Meuzza that made the poet, W B Yeats, on finding a cat asleep on his coat, quietly cut away the part beneath the creature.

The ancient Egyptians were the first to keep cats in their homes as pets and their goddess, Bastet, had the head of a cat. Such close association with a deity led to the feline race being treated with reverence, so that whenever a domestic cat died all, humans in the house were compelled by law to shave off their eyebrows to signify that they were in mourning.

9

ANIMALS WITH TOP IQs

Herbert Platt, secretary of Britian's Esperantists, used to practice the language by talking to his dog, and most owners of cats believe that they understand what is said to them. An amusing example of this appeared a few years ago in the *Seattle Times*. It was reported that when a prominent socialite in that city was rushing hither and thither preparing to receive the sixteen guests she had invited to dinner, her cat kept getting in the way until in exasperation she turned it out, crying: 'For goodness sake, Penelope, go and catch a mouse!'

All went well and then when the main dish was being served who should squeeze herself through the space under a slightly open window but Penelope, who jumped on to the table and deposited a mouse by her mistress's plate.

Right back in 1868, one finds in the learned journal, *Notes and Queries*, correspondence on the braininess of cats. A reader wrote that he was telling his neighbour about how Archbishop Whately of Dublin owned one that rang the doorbell whenever it wanted to come in. This anecdote brought out a better one from the visitor who related how the pantry window of the house he had once lived in kept being broken. Time after time, the shattered square was replaced, then, tiring of having to do this, he nailed a board over the lower row of panes. Then one night, woken by taps, as of a stone, upon glass, he looked down from his bedroom window. There was his cat, resting with her hind legs upon the sill and clinging with her left paw to the top of the board whilst, with a pebble in the other paw, she tapped an upper pane so as to break it and slip through into the pantry.

At a party I once attended where dog-lovers predominated, guests told tales to prove how exceptionally intelligent their pets were. A cocker spaniel's owner described how Suzie loved accompanying her in the car when hubby was driven to work. In fact, Suzie grew so fond of being taken out that they had to hide the car keys, for she would pounce on them and come begging for a drive. One morning, as the couple were going out together to spend the day with friends owning innumerable cats, they made it clear to the spaniel that she must remain behind.

Clearly depressed by this news, Suzie turned her back and went out of the room. Shortly afterwards, her master and mistress were about to shut the front door when they discovered that neither of them had the car keys. Turning round, they saw Suzie lying on the mat looking the picture of misery. 'Just look at the poor, poor darling!' the wife cried. 'How can we leave her behind when she's so upset? Come on Suzie, we've changed our minds!' The spaniel needed no second invitation, and leaping up she seized the car keys on which she had been lying.

An American visitor tried to cap this story with a case reported in *Newsweek* about Pal, a mongrel pup, who for almost a month had kept watch above a disused mine shaft near Joplin City in Missouri. The rumour spread that the dog was doing this because his master had fallen down the shaft, and people clamoured for the water in it to be drained. Crowds gathered to watch as for seven days, at a cost of several hundred dollars, the pumps were

114

kept busy. Then when the rescue operation ended, the pup scampered down and joyfully seized hold of a huge bone.

Trade unionism among dogs

Apsley Cherry-Garrard, the zoologist serving with Captain Scott's 'Terra Nova' expedition from 1910–12, wrote in *The Worst Journey in the World* that the most hardened trade unionist might boil with rage at the sight of a team of huskies dragging a heavy load, including their master, over the floe with every appearance of joy, but in reality they were tiring of it, and within a few days the humans in the party were to discover that 'dogs can chuck their paws in'. They would take unitedly prompt and strong action against any one of their fellows who did not do his fair share of the pulling and also against any glutton for hard work who pulled too much. A husky called Dyk was always being attacked by his team mates because whenever they stopped, he would whine and tug at his harness, so keen was he to start off again. The others resented having their rest periods cut short in this way.

Monkey talk

In apes, the vocal organs are similar to those of humans and capable of producing sounds ranging widely in pitch, quality and volume. The gorilla is noted for the volume of its voice whilst that of the gibbon and also that of the chimpanzee carries far and penetratingly. R L Garner devoted most of his life to recording, analysing and imitating these vocalisations, and provides in his books, *Gorillas and Chimpanzees*, and *Apes and Monkeys: Their Life and Their Language*, excellent evidence of the existence of vocal language in them. For several types, he describes sounds which stand as words. So definite were these vocalisations that he was able to talk to the animals.

Another distinguished naturalist, George J Romanes, wrote as far back as 1883 in his *Mental Evolution in Animals* of a chimpanzee in the London Zoo: 'This ape has learnt from her keeper the meaning of so many words and phrases that . . . he is able to explain to the animal what it is he requests her to do.'

In *The Ape in Our House* (1952), Cathy Hayes decribes how she and her husband, Keith, taught their ten months old monkey, Viki, to say 'ahhh' whenever she wanted anything. Two months later, they started teaching her to say 'mama', chosen because it was a primitive sound and frequently the first to be uttered by a baby.

Keith placed Viki on his knees with one hand round her head so that his thumb rested on her upper lip while his other fingers supported her chin. This enabled him to make her lips open and close to form the 'm'. In the morning to tempt Viki, hungry on awakening, he would hold out some food and urge her to speak. As she uttered her asking sound, he pressed her lips together, then let them part and she said 'mama'.

It was not long before Viki learnt what was expected of her and started to delay making her asking sound until Keith's fingers touched her lips. If he were slow in preparing to do this, she frequently seized his hand and placed it in the helping position. Then staring up at him, she would push her lips forward against his hand and say 'mama'. Soon Keith noticed that her lips were moving beneath his fingers, forming the word without assistance, so he gradually withdrew them to the side of her head until only the tip of his index was touching her top lip.

Finally, he took this away, too, and one morning only a fortnight after the lessons had begun, Viki spoke her first 'mama' all by herself.

When people learnt about Viki's achievement, many wanted to watch her talking. In return for some tasty offerings, she obligingly thanked her admirers with many a 'mama'. Next just before her second birthday, the Hayes taught her to say 'papa' and then 'cup', which immediately became her favourite word for as her thirst was almost unquenchable, she uttered it, according to her owners, 'perhaps a hundred times a day'.

A canine Sherlock Holmes

In the eighteenth century, there were pleasure gardens in the *Champs-Elysées* in Paris overrun by pickpockets preying on affluent visitors from the provinces. Fréville in his *Histoire des Chiens Célèbres* tells how a man from Poitou came to the capital on legal business and went with his wife for the evening to this equivalent of London's Vauxhall Gardens. Within a few minutes, expert hands had removed from his person 38 louis, a gold repeater, and a gold snuff-box set with diamonds. It was mid-summer and when his lady complained of the heat, he solicitously bought her refreshment only to discover that his purse had been stolen, as well as the watch and snuff-box. But he did not panic. A police inspector was summoned and the victim told him his name, rank, address, and asked permission to employ a servant of his to recover his missing property. This being granted, the gentleman from Poitou led the way to his coach and released from its interior a fine poodle.

'My watch, my purse, my snuff-box – all stolen,' the dog's master told it. 'Off you go – and find them!' The animal made purposefully towards a group of people and then reared up with his front paws, pressing upon the richly embroidered and gold braided coat of a man who looked like the personification of plutocracy. 'Have him searched, please,' the robbed provincial demanded. Protesting angrily, the accused was taken aside and in his pockets were found not only the repeater but two other valuable watches.

'You clever dog!' congratulated master. 'Now find my purse.' A walk round the gardens, followed by a visit to the rotunda, produced no reaction from the poodle. Then when they passed the public conveniences, the four-footed sleuth dashed inside and scratched at a closed cubicle's door, while it signalled to the others by urgently wagging its tail. They knocked. 'Is anyone inside,' the Inspector called. There was no response, and, as the door was bolted from within, he forced it open, and discovered a young man with an angelic face clad in an Abbé's robes, who protested vociferously at being disturbed while answering the call of nature. As he did so, the cleric surreptitiously removed something from a pocket and dropped it behind him, but his aim was poor and, instead of falling down into the sewer, the coin-loaded purse clinked revealingly on to the stone floor.

The imposter was marched out and frisked. The missing money was found intact, but the culprit swore that he had not stolen the diamond-adorned snuff-box. 'Then find it, my paragon among poodles!' urged its proud owner and the wonder dog, jumping up at his quarry's sleeve, shook the cuff, barking triumphantly as out rolled the snuff-box which it caught in its mouth.

'Thanks to this intelligent creature,' comments Fréville, 'two of the most wanted and elusive pick-pockets in Paris were arrested, and in their lair were found large quantities of watches, purses, swords, pistols, fans, and hundreds of handkerchiefs.'

'Old Pussy Steer'

The comment has often been made that people grow to look like their pets. This was often said of the distinguished painter, P Wilson Steer (1860-1942), who excelled equally in portraiture and landscape painting, and who was nicknamed 'Old Pussy' and had the smile of a contented cat. His niece, Miss Hamilton, had written that he liked felines because, as he used to say, they were not sycophants and provided their own boots. He made friends with strolling cats along the streets in Chelsea, talking to them in a special voice. She revealed that as a child, her uncle had his special pussies, the Duchess, a tortoiseshell, and her daughter, the Countess, followed later by Mr Pop.

As Steer preferred adult cats to kittens, when his Cheyne Walk in London black-and-white studio familiar, Mr Thomas I, died in 1906, Miss Hamilton brought from the country a replacement, Mr Thomas II, three-quarters full grown. This beautiful, gentle tabby with paws 'as soft as clouds' made Steer his fervent worshipper for eighteen years. The creature could do no harm and the only time he did any damage, by jumping up on a mantelpiece and smashing a Sèvres vase, Steer behaved as though it was the vase's fault for getting in the pet's way and certainly not his.

Miss Hamilton relates how, when her uncle began packing for his annual holiday, Mr Thomas II would become restive and distressed and afterwards mourned his absence. When three months later, master returned, he would be treated with disdain for days. A chair was reserved for him opposite Steer's. 'The great creature would leap noiselessly upon the table and contemplate anyone who sat in it with an expression of revolted patience till Steer would say, "I am afraid you are sitting in Mr Thomas's chair." '

Once Miss Hamilton took round to show her uncle a

painting she had bought which she hoped might prove to be by Monticelli. As he sat considering it, in walked Mr Thomas II and, sitting down before the picture, yawned at it. 'Well!' laughed Steer. 'So that's all old Thomas thinks of it – and I believe he's right!'

Steer was inconsolable when his pet died of influenza in 1924. George Moore in his *Conversations in Ebury Street* remembers best seeing Steer 'fat and sleek, in his armchair, his hands crossed piously over his belly's slope, his cat curled in an armchair on the other side of the fireplace, both carefully screened from the danger of draughts . . . Never did two different animals partake more closely of the same nature.'

Black Jack and Mike, the British Museum cats

The British Museum had a cat, Mike, made famous through articles written about him by the distinguished archaeologist, Sir Ernest Wallis Budge, who when the animal died on January 15, 1929, aged twenty, published his life story and that of his foster-parent. Budge began by relating how, when Sir Richard Garnett ruled over the Department of Printed Books, he was often visited by Black Jack, a handsome black creature with white shirt front and paws, fond of sitting on the Reading Room desks, who never hesitated to ask a reader to hold open both doors when he wanted to go out into the corridor. Shut in one of the newspaper rooms one Sunday, he amused himself by sharpening his claws on the bindings of volumes. As a result of the damage done, he was banished from the library. The Clerk of the Works was ordered to get rid of him but could not because Black Jack had disappeared. Two members of the staff had arranged for him to be kept in safety in a secret place where they fed him. An official report was prepared, stating that Black Jack was 'presumed dead'. Then a few weeks later, he reappeared. Everyone was delighted to see him again, and the chief officials asked no questions.

'Early in the spring of 1908,' wrote Sir Ernest, who was himself a befriender of cats, 'the Keeper of the Egyptian cat mummies in the British Museum was going down the steps of his official residence when he saw Black Jack coming towards him carrying something rather large in his mouth, which he deposited at the Keeper's feet and then turned and walked solemnly away.' It was a kitten, later known as Mike, which was taken in and cared for and grew and flourished and 'by great good luck was adopted as a pal by the two cats already in the house'.

When Mike was older, he made friends with the gatekeeper at the street entrance, and began to frequent the lodge. 'On Sunday mornings the house cat taught him to stalk pigeons in the colonnade. Mike was set to "point" like a dog, and the house cat, little by little, drove the pigeons up into a corner. They became dazed, and fell down, and then each cat seized a bird and carried it into the house uninjured. The Housekeeper took the pigeons from the cats, and in return for them gave a slice of beef or mutton and milk to each cat. The pigeons were then· taken into a little side room, and after they had eaten some maize and drunk water, they flew out of the window none the worse for their handling by the cats. The fact was that neither cat liked to eat game with dirty, sooty feathers on it; they preferred clean, cooked meat.'

As time passed, Mike, so as to keep his nocturnal amorous activities uncriticised by the Keeper's household, spent more and more time in the lodge and finally made it his permanent home. The corner shelf out of the draughts was made comfortable for him to sleep on, and he could go in and out as he pleased at all times of day and night. Sir Ernest Budge ends his account: 'The Keeper of the Mummified Cats took care to feed him during the lean years of the war, and whoever went short, Mike did not. During the last two years he was difficult to feed because of his decaying teeth, but a diet of tender meat and fish on alternate days kept him going. He preferred sole to whiting, and whiting to haddock, and sardines to herrings; for cod he had no use whatever. He owed much to the three kind-hearted gatekeepers who cooked his food for him and treated him as a man and a brother.'

'Toms' with wives in every port

The Captain of the historic aircraft carrier, the *Ark Royal*, told Beverley Nichols how they always had on board a happy lot of cats picked up by kind-hearted sailors when ashore in home ports such as Plymouth and Portsmouth. Whenever foreign shores were reached and shore leave was granted to the men, the cats, too, all rushed to queue up, with tails hoisted in the air and whiskers stiff with amorous anticipation. It was only to be expected that toms, like sailors, should have wives in every port – and the female cats, too, must have had husbands or boy friends as was made clear from the number of kittens born on the carrier following a courtesy visit to Naples.

Often when the cats went down the gangway, the Captain would tell himself: 'Well, I suppose we've said goodbye to them. I hope they'll be all right, but we shall never see them again.' But he was wrong. Whatever hour was fixed for the *Ark Royal* to sail, no cat was ever missing when departure time came. How could they know, he wondered.

TALKING TURKEY by Alison Rice (£5.95)

A lively and entertaining look at this newest holiday sensation. Travel writer and broadcaster Alison Rice has produced an up-to-date guide to the main Turkish resorts and Istanbul. Aimed at visitors new to Turkey it explains what to see, where to stay — and equally important, what to avoid. Includes basic Turkish phrases plus hints on making the best of the food, wine and shopping available.

VIVA ESPANA by Edmund Swinglehurst (£5.95)

Discover the real Spain before the bulldozers and industrialists have destroyed its natural beauty. In this comprehensive guide to Spain, Edmund Swinglehurst, travel expert and author, has provided a fascinating glimpse behind the veil of Spain to show you the heart of the countryside, its people, its culture and its way of life.

CHAMPAGNE ON A BUDGET by Patrick Delaforce (£5.95)

Champagne is probably the world's most famous wine — yet few people have discovered the sparkling region where it is produced. Wine expert and travel writer Patrick Delaforce shows you how to enjoy a trip to the Champagne region, suggests tours, visits to vineyards and gives advice on the wines worth sampling. Aimed at the independent traveller who does not wish to bust his budget this book includes lists of medium priced hotels and restaurants plus handy hints on enjoying your stay.

FRENCH RIVIERA ON A BUDGET by Patrick Delaforce (£5.95)

The land of celebrities, champagne cocktails and caviare is just waiting to be discovered. In this timely guide travel writer Patrick Delaforce shows that you don't need to break the Bank at Monte Carlo to enjoy a stay among the rich and famous along the world's famous Cote d'Azur. He lists medium priced hotels, restaurants plus plenty of advice on how to spend those sun filled days and fun filled nights.

BURGUNDY AND BEAUJOLAIS ON A BUDGET by Patrick Delaforce (£5.95)

Discover one of France's most beautiful wine regions without spending a fortune. Patrick Delaforce, wine expert and travel writer, reveals the true heart of the French countryside. Just one hour's drive from Paris lies Burgundy, famous the world over for its wines, but also one of the most beautiful and intriguing regions in France. For the gourmet there is the chance to visit the vineyards where Chablis and Beaujolais are made and sample local produce such as truffles, river fish, fine game and fresh fruits. Includes: regional tours, local wines and wine co-operatives, value for money accommodation and restaurants, places of interest, regional events.

GASCONY AND ARMAGNAC ON A BUDGET by Patrick Delaforce (£5.95)

Discover one of France's best kept secrets — the land of brandy, beaches and Basque cuisine. Wine expert and travel writer Patrick Delaforce reveals the heart of one of France's most inviting holiday locations. From the beautiful silver coast fringed with pine forests through to the inland villages, there is an alluring countryside just waiting to be discovered. Magnificent beaches, sophisticated nightlife and superb cuisine. Includes: regional tours, local wines and wine co-operatives, value for money hotels and restaurants, places of interest and regional events.

IS IT WORTH ANYTHING? by Stephen Ellis (£3.99)

Most of us have drawers filled with odds and ends. But are they worth anything? Stephen Ellis writes on the money pages of the Daily Mirror which gets thousands of letters from readers asking just that. So here for everyone who cannot bear to throw anything away 'just in case' is the book which will give most of the answers. Includes: toys, stamps, glass, jewellery, postcards, records and much more.

COOK AND HOUSEWIFE'S MANUAL by Mistress Margaret Dods (hardback £14.95)

With an introduction by Glynn Christian

Discover the world of Mistress Margaret Dods and the Cleikum Club. Mistress Dods was the founder of one of the first cookery clubs in the country and her manual, first published in 1829, includes the story of how the club was set up, over 1,000 recipes as well as hints on wine making, curing meats and making cheese. Glynn Christian says 'It is a real cookery book, a book for people who really like to eat. Comic and revelatory'. Recommended by Chat and the Glasgow Herald.

NEW FEMALE INSTRUCTOR (hardback £12.50)

First published in the 1830's the book was designed to be a practical manual aimed at turning every one of its fair readers into an intelligent and pleasing companion. It includes: dress, fashion, morals, love, courtship, duties of the married state, conduct to servants plus more than 100 pages of recipes. Lively, entertaining — the perfect gift.

THE SHARE BOOK (3rd ed) by Rosemary Burr (£5.99)

With an introduction by the Rt. Hon. Mrs. Margaret Thatcher

An up-to-date, completely revised edition of this bestselling guide to the stockmarket which has been bought by more than 50,000 people. Includes advice on every aspect of buying, selling and choosing shares. A full glossary, details of members of the Stock Exchange, Unit Trust Association and Association of Investment Trust Companies. Plus new rules on investor protection and unit trust pricing. The classic companion for anyone interested in stocks and shares.

YOUR BUSINESS IN 1992 by James Dewhurst (£6.95)

Chartered accountant, author and authority on business
management, James Dewhurst has distilled his experience
into this valuable addition to any businessman's library. What
will the much heralded internal market in Europe mean in
pratice to you and your business? The answers are inside.
Includes: setting common standards, enforcing technical
requirements, competing for orders from public bodies,
distribution services, prospects for take-overs and mergers,
new tax environment and much more.

HOMEOWNERS SURVIVAL GUIDE ed. Rosemary Burr
(£3.95)

Recommended by the Financial Times, the Sun and the
Times. Everything the homeowner needs to make the most of
his or her investment and run their home cost effectively.
Includes: choosing your home, arranging the finance, count-
down to purchase, insurance, decoration, home improvement
moving on and cost cutting ideas.